Instant Pot®
BASICS

Lisa Brady

QUAIL RIDGE PRESS
Preserving America's Food Heritage

QUAIL RIDGE PRESS

Copyright © 2019 Lisa Brady and Quail Ridge Press

Instant Pot® is a registered trademark of Instant Brands Inc. The authors and publisher are not affiliated with or endorsed by Instant Brands Inc. Use of the words Instant Pot® without the registered trademark symbol ® is only done for the sake of legibility.

Author: Lisa Brady
Cover and text design: Christian and Elise Stella
Cover and recipe photographs, food styling, and prop styling: Christian and Elise Stella
Lisa Brady photographs and photographs on pages 16, 17: Dominic Episcopo | Episcopo Studios
Other photographs, pages 6, 128, 224 and author on back cover: Chris Brady
Editorial: Linda Brock
Front cover: Instant Pot Lasagna, page 95

Library of Congress Control Number: Available by request.

ISBN: 978-1-938879-34-0
Printed in the United States of America
10 9 8 7 6 5 4 3 2 1

Instant Pot Basics was edited, designed, and manufactured by Quail Ridge Press. Quail Ridge Press is an imprint of Southwestern Publishing House, Inc., 2451 Atrium Way, Nashville, Tennessee 37214.
Southwestern Publishing House is a member of Southwestern Family of Companies, Nashville, Tennessee.

Christopher G. Capen, President, Southwestern Publishing House
Kristin Connelly, Managing Editor, Southwestern Publishing House
Kristin Stephany, Director of Partner Development, Southwestern Publishing House
Gwen and Barney McKee, Cofounders, Quail Ridge Press
Sheila Thomas, Publisher, Quail Ridge Press

quailridge.com | info@quailridge.com | 800-343-1583

Table of Contents

gluten-free

vegetarian

Introduction

Thank you for choosing my cookbook to be part of your collection of cookbooks. Whether you are new to using the Instant Pot or are already part of our Instant Pot family, I truly hope that my carefully crafted recipes and personal cooking tips will help you make delicious food that friends and family can come together and enjoy. Interactions with my QVC family and foodies inspired and helped me to pick my favorite and most sought-after tips and tricks, memorialized in this cookbook.

Cooking with my Instant Pot has changed my life. As a wife, mom, and business owner, the Instant Pot is a crucial timesaver to make quick, delicious dinners; easy breakfast foods; meal-prep lunches; decadent desserts; and wonderful party appetizers. I love that it is not only a pressure cooker but also a slow cooker, rice maker, sauté pan, and so much more, conveniently replacing many other appliances that formerly cluttered my kitchen! It's difficult not to encourage others to get an Instant Pot once you begin to incorporate it into your everyday recipes. I am excited to share my love and experiences of "Instant Potting" with you!

I have included simple, everyday recipes that will appeal to everyone who enjoys preparing delicious home-cooked meals within the constraints of a busy life. My personal commentaries are crafted to encourage the beginner as well as guide the experienced cook to get the most from their Instant Pot.

Having six children, my mom, a very talented and ingenious cook, made sure to stretch her dollar to feed all of us with hearty, home-cooked meals. Sunday dinner was always pot roast with potatoes and carrots. In one of my earliest memories, I'm watching my mom cut potatoes for her Sunday pot roast. She moved quickly, but with a graceful intention. I remember asking her, "How do you know where to cut the potatoes?" She replied, "Oh, I don't know. You just cut a small piece off the top, then just keep cutting it so they are all pretty much the same size." She explained that you want the potatoes to be the same size so that they cook evenly. With the revelation of that first secret of cooking, my fascination and excitement for the art of cooking began.

Since my childhood, my mom continued to cook everything from scratch, sometimes spending hours on one meal. When I bought her an Instant Pot pressure cooker, she was a little hesitant to use it; her old pressure cooker was overly complicated and unreliable. Eventually, I convinced her that the Instant Pot is nothing like her old pressure cooker; it is safe—with more than ten built-in safety features—and so easy to use. I told her that I use my Instant Pot almost every single day. Once she began adjusting her typical recipes to make in the Instant Pot, she was hooked. Now, my mom uses her Instant Pot all the time. Although she lives 3,000 miles away and we have a lot to catch up on over the phone, we most often discuss and share our Instant Pot recipes, meals, and tips. She is so happy to make the same delicious, home-cooked meals she has for the past sixty years but in so much less time—more time to spend with her grandkids!

In convincing my mom to become a loyal Instant Pot user, I noted the following most important benefits of using the Instant Pot:

1. Speed! You can make any recipe in much less time—up to 70 percent faster!

2. Flavor! Adding all the ingredients into the pot and cooking it under pressure infuses all the delicious seasonings and flavors together.

3. Freedom! Cooking with the Instant Pot allows you to put everything in the pot to cook and then walk away, instead of standing over the stovetop, stirring or checking on dinner every 15 minutes. This means you'll have more time to spend with friends and family.

To be honest, I'm not a fancy cook, nor am I a chef. I never attended culinary school. I am also the worst when it comes to planning meals in advance, but the Instant Pot has allowed me to significantly elevate my standard of cooking. The speed in which I can cook meals in my Instant Pot—many times with frozen ingredients—has allowed me to make healthier, heartier, and more flavorful meals that my picky family is always excited to eat! I will take any opportunity to enjoy a relaxing, home-cooked meal while conversing with my husband and children. My daughters, both living on their own, use their Instant Pots in their individual apartments. My eldest daughter, a busy working professional, meal-preps healthy lunches and dinners with her Instant Pot every Sunday evening. My younger daughter uses her Instant Pot in her college apartment to allow more time for . . . um . . . studying, right?

Not a day goes by that I am not aware of the many blessings bestowed upon me. I am so grateful for each and every blessing and appreciate them every single day! May you get as much joy reading this cookbook as I had creating it for you! God Bless.

Fondly,

Lisa

Instant Pot Basics

Whether you have picked up this book to accompany your very first Instant Pot or are just looking for a few new tricks for your favorite kitchen appliance, below are some basics that everyone should know to get the most out of this magical pressure cooker.

I have done my best to make this information (and the recipes in this book) as universal as possible, but Instant Pot has made many different models over the years. Although the basic parts and operations do not vary much by model, your Instant Pot may vary from those pictured, and some operations may be slightly different.

You should always read the manual and any documentation that came with your Instant Pot before using it.

Getting Up and Running

When you first unbox a new Instant Pot, you should follow the manual to get up and running. The basic steps you will need to perform are:

Remove and reinstall some parts of the lid, as shown in the manual, to ensure they are properly in place.

Clean the removable stainless steel insert (inner pot) with warm soapy water. Always dry the insert well before placing back into the Instant Pot!

Install the condensation collector on the back of the machine. This small plastic receptacle will catch any steam that collects around the lid. You should empty and clean this regularly.

Follow the manual to perform an Initial Test Run or "Water Test" to ensure everything is working like magic.

Cooking Under Pressure

While the Instant Pot has many functions beyond pressure cooking, it is likely that you will be using it as a pressure cooker most often. Pressure cooking is the show-stopping feature, which has made

Instant Pot a sensation that is now helping millions of people make effortless meals in a fraction of the time when cooking with conventional cooking techniques.

When cooking under pressure, liquid is converted to steam. The steam is locked in with no place to escape, creating enough pressure inside the Instant Pot to change the way the food is cooked. If you've ever heard that people at high altitude have to adjust recipes for their altitude, it's because there is lower pressure in the air, which makes food take longer to cook. Pressure cooking is the exact opposite.

The higher the pressure, the higher the boiling point of water. A higher boiling point allows food to get much hotter before it reaches that boiling point and simply boils away excess heat. It's a complicated process, but what it means is that you can make a tender pot roast in around half the time of baking it in the oven. The time saved will depend on the dish, but foods that take a longer time to cook will generally make for the most dramatic difference in cook time when cooking under pressure.

Sealing the Pressure

To cook a dish under pressure, you must ensure that the stainless steel insert is seated inside the Instant Pot. (Never cook directly in the pressure cooker without using an insert.) The silicone ring (gasket) must be properly in place under the pressure-cooking lid. You set the lid on top of the cooker and twist it clockwise until you hear a click, when it locks in place.

At this point, you ensure that the pressure release valve is set to the SEAL or SEALING position. This valve and how it operates vary by model of Instant Pot. Some require you to twist the vent or a small knob to seal; others seal automatically as you lock the lid in place. The next step would be to set the cook time.

Adding Liquids

The Instant Pot will never reach the required pressure unless you have added liquid to the stainless steel insert. This liquid is what will turn to steam and create the pressure. In general, you should always have at least 1 cup of liquid in your dish; however, this can vary by the amount of natural liquids that will be released by the food that you are cooking.

This liquid should not be too thick, or it may not create enough steam or may burn under the high heat. Ingredients that may overly thicken the cooking liquid should be added after cooking. When in doubt, always follow the recipe.

The insert has a MAX FILL line, which should always be watched to ensure that your ingredients do not fill the pot past this line. You need to leave space in the pot for the pressure to build.

Building Pressure

Once you've set the Instant Pot to "Pressure Cook," it will begin heating and slowly building pressure. This process can take anywhere from 5 minutes to 20 minutes, depending on the volume and temperature of the ingredients in the pot. A soup with a lot of broth or frozen ingredients will take far longer to build pressure than a dish with 1 cup of hot water.

Once the Instant Pot has built the right amount of pressure, it will beep, and the time you set it to cook for will display on the front panel. As time passes, it will count down to zero.

You cannot open the lid once pressure has built or any time during the cooking process. You cannot even open the lid once the cook time has elapsed. The Instant Pot's safety features keep the lid entirely locked until all pressure has been released.

Releasing the Pressure

There are two methods for releasing the pressure after cooking.

- **NATURAL RELEASE** — Once the cooking program has finished and the Instant Pot is no longer heating the ingredients, steam will stop building and will slowly begin to dissipate naturally. Eventually, all pressure will have naturally dissipated, and the lid will unlock. The time it takes for this to happen varies based on the volume of ingredients and their liquid content. A large amount of soup could take over 20 minutes, as the broth will continue to give off steam after cooking. A small amount of food could take as little as 5 minutes. Think of it as the inverse of building pressure.

- **QUICK RELEASE** — Pressure can be quickly released by opening the Instant Pot's pressure release valve to release all of the built-up steam. The method for opening this valve will vary by

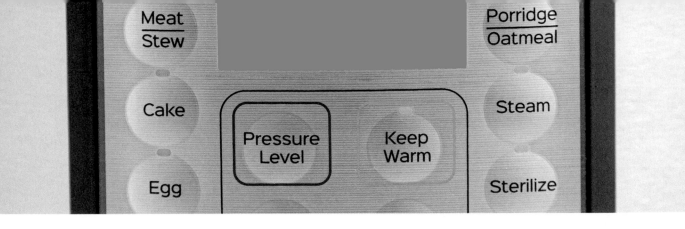

model. You will need to either press a button in or carefully twist the valve itself from SEAL to VENT or VENTING. (If you like, you can use a wooden spoon or tongs to move the valve to keep your hands away from the steam.) The valve will vent, and a large amount of steam will start to release. This steam could take as long as 2 minutes to fully release from the valve. I like to loosely drape a kitchen towel over the valve before venting. The towel will catch the steam and any splatter that may come out while venting.

If you are using the Natural Release method, understand that the ingredients inside the pot will continue to cook as the steam naturally releases. For some recipes, this could result in overcooked food. Some recipes may call for a set time of Natural Release followed by a Quick Release. Performing a Natural Release prior to a Quick Release, even for a short period of time, will lessen the amount of steam that will come out when you do the Quick Release.

When you perform a Quick Release, it rapidly changes the boiling point inside the cooker, which can cause the ingredients to lose some moisture that they would retain if the pressure was released naturally.

There is a small round metal pin beside the pressure valve on the top of the lid that will be raised when the pot is under pressure. Check this position prior to cooking so you know what the pin position is when it is under pressure and not under pressure. You will know that all pressure has been released when this pin falls. You will also hear a click as the lid unlocks for you to open it. Remember, all Instant Pot pressure cookers have nine or ten or more safety features built in. You will not be able to open the lid if it is under pressure — one of the features I LOVE about the Instant Pot!

Programs and Presets

Each model of Instant Pot comes with an assortment of programs you can activate using the buttons (or dial) on the front of the cooker. (It is important that you read the owners' manual that comes with YOUR Instant Pot in order to fully understand all the features of each program.) These programs range from entirely different cooking functions with convenient presets for HIGH or LOW pressure as well as LESS/NORMAL/MORE settings. I will explain later how awesome it is to have these preset functions. Please note: Not all programs are available on all models of Instant Pot, and some models do not include a LOW pressure mode.

There are a few things to understand about these various programs. The first is that the presets will not adjust to the food that you've put in the pot. For example, if you hit the MEAT/STEW button, the Instant Pot is not able to determine if you are cooking chicken breasts (which take around 5 minutes under High pressure) or pot roast (which takes around 75 minutes). Therefore, you must choose the pressure level (High or Low) and then choose an appropriate cook time. Once you make these selections and the Instant Pot turns on, it will memorize the setting and save it to whichever preset you were on (Less/Normal/More) when you originally set that time. Even if you turn off your machine, when you turn it back on, it will always default to this last-used setting.

The RICE and YOGURT programs are different than most of the other programs. The RICE program can be manually changed from High or Low pressure, but the Less/Normal/More settings remain at 8 minutes/12 minutes/15 minutes. These times cannot be changed or adjusted. You cannot adjust the pressure level on the YOGURT program either. You can toggle between Less/Normal/More, but on the MORE button, the panel will display "BOIL." I recommend you read the manual that comes with your machine for more specific details.

The second thing to know is how the presets are used within each of the programs. Once you choose a program, you can often choose between the presets Less/Normal/More. Out of the box, these presets are set to specific times and pressure levels; however, they can be fully adjusted to any time or pressure level by hitting the up or down arrows to change the time and the PRESSURE LEVEL button to change between High and Low pressure. The nice thing about this is that most programs will memorize three different settings for three of your most cooked dishes.

In each program, once you have adjusted the Less/Normal/More time preset and the High/Low pressure setting, the Instant Pot will remember that preset until the next time you adjust it. They are truly like programming your favorite stations on a car radio. You can use them to save the cook times of recipes you prepare often.

You will notice that in all my recipes, I do not mention Less/Normal/More presets. This is because the Instant Pot remembers the last setting used, and your last setting for a program may not be my last setting for a program. It's entirely possible that your Meat/Stew program on the Less preset is set to 80 minutes at High pressure and my Less preset could be set to 20 minutes on Low pressure. It's truly just the last time and pressure you set on each preset. As you prepare the recipes in this book, always double-check the cook time and pressure level for the program that you are on to ensure it matches the time and pressure level for the recipe.

Pressure Cooking Programs

Most of the Instant Pot programs cook under pressure. These programs are extremely similar to each other when it comes to the final results. In fact, if your Instant Pot does not have a specific button/program that is used within a recipe, simply use the manual PRESSURE COOK button instead and then set the pressure level and time directed in the recipe. Most programs have three customizable time levels; however, you have the ability to add or subtract time from any of these levels.

The pressure-cooking programs named after specific foods are provided as a convenience so you can preset each program without having to take too much time adjusting the time to cook and the pressure levels every time you cook. The temperature will vary based only on whether you have selected High or Low pressure, not by the specific program selected. If you have the program on your Instant Pot for the food you are cooking, use it; but, if not, you will still achieve the same result if you cook using the manual mode.

- **Pressure Cook** — This is known as the MANUAL MODE. It can be set to High or Low pressure. You can choose the Less/Normal/More preset to have three different preset settings in this program. You may also use this program for cooking any food that doesn't fit into any specific program.

- **Soup/Broth** — In this program, you can select Less/Normal/More and High/Low pressure. Due to the high liquid content, I recommend using a Natural Release for this program.

- **Meat/Stew** — In this program, you can select Less/Normal/More and High/Low pressure. Allow meats to rest after cooking to absorb all the juices.

- **Bean/Grain** — In this program, you can select Less/Normal/More and High/Low pressure.

- **Cake** — This program is intended for making cakes in a cake pan above a water bath. Do not cook a cake directly in the Instant Pot insert! In this program, you can select Less/Normal/More and High/Low pressure.

- **Egg** — This program allows you to select Less/Normal/More and High/Low pressure. With the factory presets, Less is intended for soft–boiled eggs, Normal is intended for medium-boiled eggs, and More is intended for hard-boiled eggs.

After cooking, plunge eggs into an ice bath to prevent overcooking.

• **Porridge/Oatmeal** — In this program, you can select Less/Normal/More and High/Low pressure. I highly recommend NOT using the Quick Release method in this program, as the thick liquid can splatter and block the pressure release valve. Allow time for a Natural Release when selecting this program.

• **Steam** — In this program, you can select Less/Normal/More and High/Low pressure. I recommend you remove steamed vegetables immediately to prevent overcooking. Even if the timer has counted down, food will continue to cook if the lid remains on.

• **Sterilize** — This program is suitable for tempered glass and heat-resistant plastics. You can sterilize baby bottles, jars, or utensils in this program.

The Rice Program

The RICE program is technically a pressure-cooking setting, as it prepares rice quickly under pressure; but it is more unique than the other programs, as it is fully automatic. The Less/Normal/More presets on this program will never change, and there is no need to adjust the time. LESS is for tender but firm rice, NORMAL is for fully tender rice, and MORE is for softer rice.

The RICE program is only meant for cooking any variety of white rice and is especially good with long grain varieties. For more tips on cooking rice, see Perfect White or Brown Rice (recipe page 187).

The Slow Cook Program

The SLOW COOK program will turn your Instant Pot into a slow cooker. In this program, you can select Less/Normal/More. LESS equates to the LOW setting on a common slow cooker, NORMAL equates to the MEDIUM setting on a common slow cooker, and MORE equates to the HIGH setting on a common slow cooker. Most common slow cookers only have two temperatures, so oftentimes slow-cooking recipes do not refer to a "normal" temperature setting.

While you can usually achieve similar results in far less time by pressure cooking, slow cooking can be convenient for times when you want to start a meal cooking far in advance. It also can be convenient for recipes that may have a lot of dairy or very delicate ingredients that may break down under high pressure. I like to use the Slow Cook program to keep certain dishes hot (like warm dips), rather than use the KEEP WARM button. When slow cooking in the Instant Pot, it is best to cover the pot with a glass lid. Never slow cook with the main lid locked in place and the pressure valve closed!

The Yogurt Program

The YOGURT program provides all the steps necessary to make your own yogurt, including pasteurizing the milk at a high temperature before fermenting it at a low temperature for several hours. For step-by-step directions on using the Yogurt program to make Homemade Yogurt, see my recipe on page 35.

Sautéing with the Instant Pot

The SAUTÉ button on your Instant Pot will turn your cooker into an electric skillet, which will allow you to brown meats and vegetables or even cook an entire dish, just as you would on the stovetop.

There are three non-programmable Sauté presets, Less/Normal/More, which are equal to Low/Medium/High on the stovetop. To start sautéing, simply hit the SAUTÉ button until your desired preset is selected. It will beep and begin to preheat. You should let the insert preheat for 2 minutes before adding oil or ingredients (similar to if you are preheating your pan on the stovetop). In this program, Less is intended for simmering and reducing, Normal is intended for pan searing or sautéing, and More is intended for stir frying or browning.

The recipes in this book use the More preset unless otherwise noted. I typically do all of my browning and sautéing on this preset and only switch to a lower preset in the middle of cooking if food begins to brown too quickly. The Less preset can come in handy if you are working with ingredients that are prone to burning, such as sugar or milk.

Browning to Build Flavors

As you flip through this cookbook, you may notice that a majority of the recipes will start with browning meat or sautéing vegetables before cooking them under pressure. The culinary term I use most often is "fond," the French word for base or foundation. These are the delicious brown bits that get stuck to the bottom of your pan when you are sautéing meat. Browning ingredients, especially meat, causes the "Maillard Reaction," which not only gives the food some color but also causes entirely new flavor compounds to come out of it. (Please be sure to read below about deglazing. This step is crucial when browning meats.) This is why roasted (or even sautéed) garlic has an entirely different flavor than raw garlic. It is also why caramelized onions taste so much better than boiled onions. The Maillard Reaction also brings out the natural sugars that

are present in almost every food we eat, adding additional depth via sweetness—another reason why roasted garlic and caramelized onions are so delicious. . . . They are naturally sweet.

Whether baking, grilling, or pan frying, most conventional methods of cooking meat will create at least some browning. As pressure cooking is a steam environment that does not need to rely on direct heat to cook, you are unlikely to have any foods brown on their own under pressure. This is why it is always good to brown meat and sauté aromatics (onions, garlic, celery) before cooking under pressure. The great news is that pressure cooking will then lock those new flavors in and infuse them into everything else in the dish.

Can you skip the browning step? Most of the time you can, but the results will not be as flavorful and will not look as good as they could have. Garlic, onions, and some spices will also retain their stronger, raw flavors. I skip the browning when cooking from frozen meats, and I still get meals that my family loves.

Ground beef and bacon are two foods that should always be browned before cooking under pressure. If not browned, ground beef will soak up liquid as it cooks and almost melt into the cooking liquid, and bacon will become rubbery.

Deglazing the Insert

When browning ingredients (whether in the Instant Pot or otherwise), you MUST always, always, always deglaze the pot, as bits of what you are browning are naturally going to stick. As pressure cooking requires liquid to come up to pressure, you are almost always going to have some liquid from the recipe that you can pour into the insert to help release any browned bits from the bottom of the insert. Pour the liquid in while the insert is still hot and use a spatula or Spurtle to thoroughly scrape the bottom until it is entirely clear of any browning. This will also release a ton of flavor into your cooking liquid to make a better final dish. (See below for BURN message information. If you do not deglaze your insert, you are sure to see this message!)

The Burn Warning

The Instant Pot is equipped with a sensor that can tell if something is starting to burn to the bottom of the insert. This is incredibly helpful when cooking under pressure, as you cannot open the lid to check on your food without having to release all the pressure, only to have to re-pressurize to finish the cooking process.

If the Instant Pot senses something burning, it will stop the current program and display a message that reads "FOOD BURN" or simply "BURN" on the display panel. If you ever see this message, lightly place a kitchen towel over the pressure valve and open it to begin releasing the pressure. Once all the pressure has released, check the bottom of the insert for burnt food and scrape any and all of it away before attempting to finish cooking. It is a good idea to stir in some additional liquid before attempting to finish cooking the dish under pressure.

The Instant Pot's burn sensor is notoriously sensitive, but that's actually a very good thing. It often is triggered when food is only browning to the bottom of the insert, minutes before it would actually start burning. This gives you time to correct the problem and actually save your meal.

That being said, as the sensor is so sensitive, you must be diligent about deglazing the insert before cooking under pressure. More often than not, the BURN warning will appear because food got stuck on the bottom during the browning process.

Cooking Sous Vide

One of the most exciting programs to start appearing on new models of the Instant Pot is the SOUS VIDE program. Sous vide is French for "under vacuum" and has been used as a method of cooking in fine-dining restaurants for decades. Just a few years ago, it would have cost thousands of dollars to buy a traditional sous vide immersion circulator, but now it is just one of the many Instant Pot programs.

Sous vide cooking is done in a water bath set to a very precise, often low temperature. You place the food in a vacuum-seal bag (such as the FoodSaver) and remove all air before submerging in the water to cook.

If you are not familiar with the sous vide method, it can be hard to fully appreciate what makes it different from other cooking methods. Think of the water bath like a hot tub that is very hot when you first step in, but then, after a short while, you get used to the water and are able to stay in for a long period of time. That is what is happening inside the Instant Pot. Under water that is a set temperature, heat doesn't continue building; it simply stays that exact temperature. It is impossible for food to overcook, as the temperature of the food hits the water's temperature and cannot build any further. It just acclimates to the water.

Why this is such an amazing thing is that, especially for meat, the doneness is determined by temperature, not time.

Medium rare steak is 135°F., but you don't set your grill or oven to 135°F to cook it. You set it much, much higher, which means the temperature of the steak will continue rising and rising as it cooks, so you must pay close attention. When cooking sous vide, you set the water to be exactly the 135°F that you want the finished steak. Then you vacuum seal the steak and submerge it. It will take around an hour to reach the temperature of the water and be perfectly medium rare. If you leave the steak in the water—cooking sous vide—for three more hours, it will be the exact same medium rare. It simply cannot overcook. Heat isn't building; it is simply holding steady.

While foods do not go past the temperature of the water, the natural proteins in the food do break down as time goes on (the same way that they break down when cooking under pressure), making for extremely tender meat. Many sous vide recipes will recommend a range for the cook time. The low end of this range is when the meat will have come up to the final temperature, and you can stop the cooking at that point if you wish. The high end of this range is the time when the meat may start to get unnaturally tender, so you will not want to cook longer than that time.

Do You Need a Vacuum Sealer?

You can sous vide with freezer-grade storage bags, but you must be sure the bag is completely sealed. I highly recommend using a FoodSaver vacuum-sealed bag. There is nothing worse than coming back to check on your food after a few hours and finding that the bag leaked and spoiled your dinner! For ordinary food storage bags, place the food in the bag and then slowly dip into water with the seal open and above the water line until the water pushes most of the air out of the bag. Seal the bag and submerge. You may need to place a heavy plate atop the bag to keep it submerged.

Start Cooking Sous Vide

To cook sous vide, prepare your water bath first, as this could take 20 to 50 minutes to reach temperature. You can use this time to prepare your food.

- Place a steam rack in the bottom of the stainless steel inner pot and fill with warm water up to the PC MAX line (2/3 full)—no higher.
- Place inner pot in the cooker base and place

lid on to keep heat in. Lock the lid in place, but be sure to open the pressure valve to the VENT position. (You may also use a glass lid.) Using a lid will ensure the water stays insulated and an even temperature, while reducing evaporation.

- Press SOUS VIDE once, then press "+" or "-" to select the temperature.
- Press SOUS VIDE a second time and press "+" or "-" to set the time. Cooker will beep and ON will appear on the front panel while preheating. Once it reaches temperature, the timer will begin counting down.
- Prepare your food in a vacuum-sealed bag, and vacuum seal it to remove the air.
- Once the water has preheated and the timer appears on the front panel, you may submerge your sealed bag in the water. Replace the lid on the cooker. The timer will count down as the food is cooking.

Browning After Sous Vide

It is best to brown meat after it has been cooked sous vide to make for a more appetizing color and deeper flavor. Remove the cooked meat from the vacuum bag and pat dry with paper towels. Brown in a very hot Instant Pot set to SAUTÉ or on a stovetop or grill. You want to brown the meat as quickly as possible and get it off the heat, as it was already perfectly cooked before browning.

Instant Pot Accu Slim

If your Instant Pot does not have a SOUS VIDE program, Instant Pot does offer an accessory for sous vide cooking, called the Accu Slim. This device can be lowered into your Instant Pot insert (or any pot) to heat the water and circulate it at the same time. Because the water is constantly circulating, it does not require a lid on the cooker to keep things insulated.

Must-Have Accessories

There are some accessories every Instant Pot owner should have. They will allow you to expand the types of recipes you can prepare and even start "baking" desserts under pressure.

Steam Rack

Most Instant Pot models will come with a steam rack in the box. It's simply indispensable and Instant Pot knows that! Steam racks are simply a surface to raise food or baking dishes above the water line, allowing them to steam. The best steam racks have handles to easily lower and lift food in and out of the pot.

Steam Basket

Steam baskets are handy for steaming larger amounts of ingredients or smaller ingredients, especially vegetables.

Glass Lid

Instant Pot makes a glass lid, which you can use when you aren't cooking under pressure. This is great for quicker access and seeing how your meal is cooking. This is often a separate purchase and is not a standard accessory with most Instant Pots.

An Extra Insert

If you cook in your Instant Pot every day as I do, there's no better investment than a second insert to cook in. They're reasonably priced and allow you to use your cooker while the other insert is in the dishwasher or is in the refrigerator storing leftovers.

7-inch Springform Pan

This will be your most-used cake pan inside the Instant Pot and not just for making cakes. I also use this pan for making pies, quiches, bread pudding, and even lasagna! (More times than not, you will be covering this pan with foil to prevent steam from getting into your dish.)

6-ounce Ramekins

A set of four ramekins is great for making mini desserts or egg dishes.

Egg Bite Mold

This silicone mold is used to make delicious Egg Bites and also can be used to make even smaller desserts than the ramekins.

7-inch Bundt Pan

This pan can be used to make my Tropical Paradise Cake (recipe page 207) but also can be used for bread puddings. I also love to use Anchor Hocking Glass Storage Bowls. They can take the heat and are pretty enough to bring right to the table.

Extra Silicone Rings

The silicone ring (or gasket) inside the lid ensures that the pot remains airtight to build pressure. It also tends to absorb strong flavors. It's a good idea to have at least 2 silicone rings: one for savory dishes and one for sweet.

Lisa's Favorite Things

Here are the top six items I have in my kitchen! I had to do some digging to see if they are even still available. I did not want to tell you my favorites and then not have you be able to find them! There is no advantage to me telling you about these items, other than that I wanted to share with you my favorite kitchen gadgets, which I own and use all the time.

Mad Hungry Spurtles | The combination of a spoon and a spatula makes this one of the best kitchen tools for stirring, scraping, spreading, scooping, and serving. I love the natural wood as well as all the fun colors they come in! It adds a nice pop of color in my kitchen!

Rapid Slicer | Not only is this great for bagels (the number one reason people take trips to the ER when using a knife), but also it is fantastic for slicing perfectly thin chicken breasts (for even cooking results), tomatoes, olives, and other fruits and veggies in seconds. I find that when I slice things like grapes for my salad, it actually seems to open up the flavor of the grapes. The Rapid Slicer is the newest kitchen gadget in my arsenal, and I love it!

FoodSaver | If you do not have a FoodSaver Vacuum Sealing System, you need to get one now! No home should be without it! Trust me on this one. Whatever you eat will eventually go bad if you don't eat it soon enough—whether it is veggies, fruits, meats, cheese, or cookies; it does not matter. If you are not vacuum sealing it to extend the shelf life up to 5 times longer, you are losing money. You know the saying: "cash in the trash!" This will happen unless you grocery shop every day, and who does that?

Anchor Hocking Glass Storage Set | I did not realize that my mom has been using Anchor Hocking bowls for years. These glass bowls with TrueSeal Lids are awesome. I love making my lasagna in my 7-cup dish. It fits perfectly in the Instant Pot, and the embossed glass is so pretty to bring right to the table. And they are microwave and dishwasher safe. How cool is that?

Kuhn Rikon Wrap Dispenser | This is another must-have for your kitchen. You will never have to worry about plastic wrap getting all messed up again. It stores it and cuts it. Nonslip feet and silicone-type grippers keep it from moving around. I used one like this when I cooked in a restaurant, but it was a huge commercial unit. This is for the at-home cook. I bought mine in a set of two, one for plastic wrap and one for foil. Anytime someone sees me using it, they say, "Wow, that's cool!"

Kuhn Rikon Pull Chop Food Chopper | Yes, it's another Kuhn Rikon item! My good friend MCM would be so happy! This is the perfect gadget for chopping up fruits and veggies. It is so easy and fast. It's especially great if you are not very comfortable with a knife. This dices beautifully, too.

Breakfast and Brunch

pressure cook

(V) Blueberry French Toast Casserole, 21

(🌾) (V) White Pizza Egg White Frittata, 22

(🌾) (V) Homemade Applesauce, 23

Morning Egg Bites, 25

(🌾) (V) Apple, Cinnamon, and Raisin Steel-Cut Oats, 26

(🌾) (V) Pesto Egg Cups, 27

(🌾) (V) Raspberry Preserves, 29

(🌾) Ham, Broccoli, and Cheddar Quiche, 30

Sausage and Pepper Strata, 31

sauté

Kielbasa and Home Fry Hash, 33

yogurt

(🌾) (V) Homemade Yogurt, 35

Blueberry French Toast Casserole

This breakfast bread pudding is made with buttery brioche bread, just as you'd use for classic French toast. Blueberries, maple syrup, and a hint of cinnamon bring even more breakfast flavors to a dish that can feed the whole family.

Ingredients

Nonstick cooking spray

5 large eggs

1½ cups whole milk

3 tablespoons pure maple syrup

2 tablespoons sugar

¼ teaspoon vanilla extract

¼ teaspoon ground cinnamon

Pinch salt

5 thick slices brioche bread, coarsely chopped

1 cup blueberries

ACCESSORIES

7-inch springform pan

PRESSURE COOK | HIGH PRESSURE | 45 MINUTES | NATURAL RELEASE

1 Spray a 7-inch springform pan with nonstick cooking spray. Fully wrap the outside and bottom of the pan with aluminum foil to prevent leaking from the bottom as you fill the pan.

2 In a large mixing bowl, whisk together eggs, milk, maple syrup, sugar, vanilla extract, cinnamon, and salt.

3 Fold bread and blueberries into the egg mixture. For best results, let stand 15 minutes.

4 Transfer the bread and egg mixture to the prepared pan and cover tightly with aluminum foil.

5 Pour 1 cup of water into the Instant Pot insert. Set the springform pan on a steam rack and lower into the insert. Secure lid and seal pressure release vent.

6 Set Instant Pot to PRESSURE COOK on HIGH for 45 minutes.

7 Once cook time has elapsed, let the pressure release through NATURAL RELEASE.

8 Remove aluminum foil and let cool 5 minutes before unlocking springform pan and slicing to serve.

Just the Basics

The blueberries in this dish like to sink to the bottom, so it is best to transfer the bread mixture into the pan a little at a time, scooping from the bottom to ensure you are evenly dispersing the blueberries.

Make it My Way

I like to serve this topped with powdered sugar and drizzled with additional maple syrup. For a dessert, I like to mix a small handful of chocolate chips into the pudding before cooking and then top with vanilla ice cream.

Notes

White Pizza Egg White Frittata

This deep-dish egg white frittata has all of the flavors you'd find on a white pizza: ricotta cheese, spinach, and a good amount of garlic. It's all topped off with a layer of mozzarella cheese.

BREAKFAST

Ingredients

Nonstick cooking spray

8 large egg whites

³/₄ cup ricotta cheese

1 tablespoon minced garlic

¹/₂ teaspoon dried oregano

¹/₂ teaspoon salt

¹/₄ teaspoon pepper

¹/₂ cup frozen chopped spinach, thawed and drained well

¹/₂ cup mozzarella cheese

ACCESSORIES

7-inch springform pan

PRESSURE COOK | HIGH PRESSURE | 25 MINUTES | NATURAL RELEASE

1 Spray a 7-inch springform pan with nonstick cooking spray. Fully wrap the outside and bottom of the pan with aluminum foil to prevent leaking from the bottom as you fill the pan.

2 In a mixing bowl, whisk together egg whites, ricotta cheese, garlic, oregano, salt, and pepper.

3 Fold in chopped spinach and then pour into the prepared pan. Top with the mozzarella cheese. Cover tightly with aluminum foil.

4 Pour 1 cup of water into the Instant Pot insert. Place wrapped springform pan on a steam rack and lower into the insert. Secure lid and seal pressure release vent.

5 Set Instant Pot to PRESSURE COOK on HIGH for 25 minutes.

6 Once cook time has elapsed, let the pressure release through NATURAL RELEASE for 10 minutes before quick releasing any remaining pressure.

7 Remove aluminum foil and let rest 3 minutes before unlocking springform pan and slicing to serve.

Just the Basics

For even more pizza flavor, you can serve this topped with a dollop of warmed pizza sauce.

Notes

Homemade Applesauce

Applesauce is one of my daughter's favorite snacks, and making it fresh allows me to know exactly what is in it! The Instant Pot has encouraged me to make things I never would have attempted to make in the past. I would have never thought to make my own applesauce, but the results are absolutely worth it.

Ingredients

1½ pounds Granny Smith apples

1½ pounds Gala apples

½ cup water

¼ cup light brown sugar

1 cinnamon stick

PORRIDGE | HIGH PRESSURE | 5 MINUTES | NATURAL RELEASE

1 Peel, core, and roughly chop the apples into large pieces, adding to the Instant Pot insert as you go.

2 Pour water over apples and sprinkle the sugar over the top without stirring. Stick the cinnamon stick down into the center of the apples.

3 Secure lid and seal pressure release vent.

4 Set Instant Pot to PORRIDGE on HIGH pressure for 5 minutes.

5 Once cook time has elapsed, let the pressure release through NATURAL RELEASE.

6 Remove cinnamon stick and use a potato masher to mash the apples until they've reached your desired consistency. For smoother applesauce, transfer to a food processor or blender and pulse only a few times until mostly smooth.

Make it My Way

This is only lightly sweetened and, depending on the natural sweetness of the apples, you may wish to sweeten with additional sugar or any sweetener of your choice after cooking.

Just the Basics

Any variety of apples can be used to make this, but firm apples work the best. Very soft apples (such as McIntosh) are not recommended.

Notes

Morning Egg Bites

Egg bites are some of the simplest and most addictive things (especially when they have Cheddar cheese and bacon) you can make in your Instant Pot. I used to make this exact recipe in ramekins before they started making dedicated silicone "egg bite molds." Now, they come out even better than ever.

Ingredients

Nonstick cooking spray

5 strips bacon, cooked
 and crumbled

1 1/2 tablespoons chopped chives

5 large eggs

1/3 cup shredded sharp
 Cheddar cheese

1/4 cup heavy cream

1/4 teaspoon salt

1/8 teaspoon white
 pepper, optional

ACCESSORIES

Egg bite mold

PRESSURE COOK | HIGH PRESSURE | 10 MINUTES | NATURAL RELEASE

1. Place a steam rack in the Instant Pot insert and pour in 1 cup of water. Spray a silicone egg bite mold with nonstick cooking spray.

2. Evenly distribute the bacon and chives between each cup of the egg bite mold.

3. In a blender or food processor, combine eggs, Cheddar cheese, cream, salt, and pepper and blend just until smooth.

4. Divide the egg mixture evenly among the cups of the egg bite mold. Wrap tightly in aluminum foil and place over steam rack.

5. Secure lid and seal pressure release vent.

6. Set Instant Pot to PRESSURE COOK on HIGH for 10 minutes.

7. Once cook time has elapsed, let the pressure release through NATURAL RELEASE for 5 minutes before carefully quick releasing any remaining pressure.

Make it My Way

I use white pepper in these because I've found that black pepper sinks to the bottom and accumulates there in one place. If you don't have white pepper, you can simply omit it entirely.

Just the Basics

Most silicone egg bite molds come with a plastic cover. Do not use this cover inside the Instant Pot as it is meant only for storage and is not heatproof!

Notes

Apple, Cinnamon, and Raisin Steel-Cut Oats

Steel-cut oats are much heartier and far less processed than quick-cooking or even regular "old-fashioned" oats, but few people take the time to prepare them. Thankfully, the Instant Pot allows you to prepare this more natural version of a favorite in less time than it would take to prepare regular oats on the stove. The best thing about this recipe is that you put everything in the Instant Pot and walk away! You don't have to stand at the stove and stir, worry about a boil over, or deal with oats burning to the bottom of a pan.

Ingredients

1 cup steel-cut oats

3 cups water

1 small apple, chopped

1/2 cup raisins

1/4 cup pure maple syrup

1/4 teaspoon ground cinnamon

Milk, optional

PORRIDGE | HIGH PRESSURE | 4 MINUTES | NATURAL RELEASE

1 In the Instant Pot insert, stir to combine oats, water, apple, raisins, maple syrup, and cinnamon.

2 Secure lid and seal pressure release vent.

3 Set Instant Pot to PORRIDGE on HIGH pressure for 4 minutes.

4 Once cook time has elapsed, let the pressure release through NATURAL RELEASE.

5 Serve as is or drizzled with milk for added creaminess.

Make it My Way

This is how I love to prepare my oats; however, you can omit the apple, raisins, maple syrup, and cinnamon to make plain oats to top with your favorite ingredients. They can even be seasoned with salt and pepper and topped with savory ingredients for a unique lunch.

Just the Basics

This makes a large batch of oats that can be refrigerated for up to 3 days. To reheat, microwave for 2 minutes.

Notes

Pesto Egg Cups

Whole eggs are cooked with pesto sauce in single-serving ramekins in this quick and easy breakfast recipe. Topping them with Parmesan cheese brings more flavor, while a sprinkling of diced pimentos adds a bit of color.

Ingredients

Nonstick cooking spray

4 tablespoons prepared basil pesto

4 large eggs

Salt and pepper

2 tablespoons diced pimentos

4 tablespoons shredded Parmesan cheese

ACCESSORIES

4 (6-ounce) ramekins

PRESSURE COOK | LOW PRESSURE | 2 MINUTES | QUICK RELEASE

1 Spray ramekins with nonstick cooking spray.

2 Spread a tablespoon of pesto over the bottom of each ramekin and then crack a whole egg over top. Season lightly with salt and pepper.

3 Sprinkle ½ tablespoon of diced pimentos and 1 tablespoon of Parmesan cheese over each egg.

4 Fully wrap each ramekin in aluminum foil.

5 Pour 1 cup of water into the Instant Pot insert. Place wrapped ramekins on a steam rack and lower into the insert. Secure lid and seal pressure release vent.

6 Set Instant Pot to PRESSURE COOK on LOW for 2 minutes.

7 Once cook time has elapsed, carefully perform a QUICK RELEASE of the pressure.

8 Quickly remove the steam rack with ramekins and check one for doneness. If the whites are not firm, rewrap, set steam rack back in Instant Pot, and set to SAUTÉ. Secure lid with pressure vent open and let cook just 1 minute. (The beauty of the Instant Pot is even if something is not cooked all the way, you just add more time and cook it some more!)

Just the Basics

To fit 4 ramekins in the Instant Pot at the same time, you may have to place 3 of them in a triangular pattern with the fourth sitting atop where those intersect.

Make it My Way

I keep this simple by buying already prepared pesto sauce at my local grocery store.

Notes

Raspberry Preserves

These homemade preserves are simple to make and taste far fresher than anything you'd buy in a jar. Cornstarch is used to thicken rather than fruit pectin, as it ensures perfect results every time without having to purchase any special ingredients. I just love making this to serve alongside Brie cheese!

Ingredients

24 ounces frozen raspberries

2 tablespoons water

1 tablespoon lemon juice

3/4 cup sugar

2 1/2 tablespoons cornstarch

3 tablespoons water

PRESSURE COOK | HIGH PRESSURE | 4 MINUTES | NATURAL RELEASE

1 Place raspberries, 2 tablespoons water, and lemon juice in the Instant Pot insert. While this seems like very little liquid, the raspberries will release plenty of liquid as the pot comes up to pressure.

2 Secure lid and seal pressure release vent.

3 Set Instant Pot to PRESSURE COOK on HIGH for 4 minutes.

4 Once cook time has elapsed, let the pressure release through NATURAL RELEASE.

5 Set Instant Pot to SAUTÉ and stir in sugar.

6 Whisk cornstarch into 3 tablespoons of cold water and, stirring constantly, add to the cooked raspberries. Bring up to a simmer and stir, just until thickened. Immediately turn off cooker and remove insert from cooker to prevent further cooking or burning. You may wish to stir in additional sugar to taste.

7 Cover and refrigerate at least 1 hour before serving.

Make it My Way

While raspberries are my favorite, you can use this same method to make blueberry, blackberry, or strawberry preserves.

Just the Basics

Make sure the pressure has fully released naturally before opening the pressure release vent, as the cooked raspberries will be very thick and could splatter from the vent if they are still under pressure.

Notes

Ham, Broccoli, and Cheddar Quiche

This crustless and always smooth quiche is packed with broccoli, ham, and plenty of sharp Cheddar cheese. Serve it warm or chilled. It can even be prepped, wrapped, and refrigerated the night before for a breakfast you can just set and forget.

BREAKFAST

Ingredients

Nonstick cooking spray

1¼ cups shredded sharp Cheddar cheese

1 cup chopped broccoli florets

¾ cup diced ham

2 tablespoons finely diced white onion

6 large eggs

¼ cup heavy cream

¼ cup milk

½ teaspoon salt

¼ teaspoon pepper

ACCESSORIES

7-inch springform pan

PRESSURE COOK | HIGH PRESSURE | 25 MINUTES | NATURAL RELEASE

1 Spray a 7-inch springform pan with nonstick cooking spray.

2 Place the Cheddar cheese, broccoli, ham, and onion in the springform pan and toss to combine.

3 In a mixing bowl, whisk together all remaining ingredients. Pour over ingredients in the springform pan and gently stir.

4 Fully wrap and cover the springform pan in aluminum foil to prevent any water from seeping into the bottom of the pan.

5 Pour 1 cup of water into the Instant Pot insert. Place wrapped springform pan on a steam rack and lower into the insert. Secure lid and seal pressure release vent.

6 Set Instant Pot to PRESSURE COOK on HIGH for 25 minutes.

7 Once cook time has elapsed, let the pressure release through NATURAL RELEASE.

8 Remove Instant Pot lid and let rest in cooker an additional 5 minutes before slicing to serve.

Just the Basics

Uncooked fresh broccoli works best in this recipe, but thawed frozen broccoli can be used in a pinch, as long as you squeeze out any excess water.

Notes _____

_____

Sausage and Pepper Strata

A strata is a savory egg casserole with bread and, in this case, breakfast sausage, Cheddar cheese, peppers, and onions. Prep it the night before for a breakfast you can set and forget the next morning.

Ingredients

Nonstick cooking spray

5 large eggs

$3/4$ cup whole milk

$1/3$ cup heavy cream

$1/2$ teaspoon salt

$1/4$ teaspoon pepper

$1/4$ teaspoon garlic powder

4 thick slices hearty bread, coarsely chopped

6 links fully-cooked breakfast sausage, chopped

$3/4$ shredded sharp Cheddar cheese

$2/3$ cup frozen chopped peppers and onions, thawed

ACCESSORIES

7-inch springform pan

PRESSURE COOK | HIGH PRESSURE | 45 MINUTES | NATURAL RELEASE

1 Spray a 7-inch springform pan with nonstick cooking spray. Fully wrap the outside and bottom of the pan to prevent leaking from the bottom as you fill the pan.

2 In a large mixing bowl, whisk together eggs, milk, heavy cream, salt, pepper, and garlic powder.

3 Fold bread, sausage, Cheddar cheese, and peppers and onions into the egg mixture to create the strata batter. For best results, let stand 15 minutes.

4 Press the strata batter into the prepared pan and cover tightly with aluminum foil.

5 Pour 1 cup of water into the Instant Pot insert. Set the springform pan on a steam rack and lower into the insert. Secure lid and seal pressure release vent.

6 Set Instant Pot to PRESSURE COOK on HIGH for 45 minutes.

7 Once cook time has elapsed, let the pressure release through NATURAL RELEASE.

8 Let cool 10 minutes before slicing to serve.

Just the Basics

This can be made from scratch by starting with 6 raw sausage links, chopped; $1/2$ cup diced yellow onion; and $1/2$ cup diced bell pepper. Sauté in 1 tablespoon of vegetable oil until sausage is cooked and vegetables are soft. Drain and cool before assembling the strata.

Notes

Kielbasa and Home Fry Hash

You've just got to serve this breakfast hash topped with a perfectly fried egg! I've made this unique by using smoked kielbasa rather than any variety of traditional breakfast sausage, but I've also kept it quick and easy by opting for frozen diced hash browns so that there's no need to painstakingly dice potatoes by hand. I use my trusted Kuhn Rikon chopper to quickly chop the other ingredients.

Ingredients

3 tablespoons vegetable oil

14 ounces smoked kielbasa sausage, chopped

1 small yellow onion, diced

1/2 red bell pepper, diced

2 teaspoons minced garlic

1 tablespoon smoked paprika

1/2 teaspoon onion powder

1/4 cup chicken stock

4 cups frozen diced hash brown potatoes

2 tablespoons chopped fresh parsley

Salt and pepper to taste

SAUTÉ | 15 MINUTES

1 Preheat the Instant Pot insert on SAUTÉ. Add vegetable oil and heat until it thins out.

2 Add sausage and cook until lightly browned.

3 Add onion, bell pepper, garlic, smoked paprika, and onion powder and sauté an additional 3 minutes before deglazing the pot with the chicken stock.

4 Stir in potatoes and sauté until potatoes are tender, about 7 minutes.

5 Stir in chopped parsley and season with salt and pepper to taste before serving.

Make it My Way

This is also great when made with smoked chicken sausage, especially the kind with apples in it, as it has a light cinnamon flavor that is perfect for breakfast.

Just the Basics

If you find the home fries sticking to the bottom of the insert, add additional chicken stock and scrape the bottom to ensure that nothing burns.

Notes

Homemade Yogurt

Making the freshest-tasting homemade yogurt can be done in only a few minutes of actual prep work, using your choice of milk (the higher the milk fat, the thicker the finished yogurt will be). While it may seem counterintuitive, homemade yogurt needs to start with a small amount of store-bought yogurt to get the active cultures into the milk to start their process. After your first batch, you can use that homemade yogurt to start your next batch and so on.

Ingredients

½ gallon milk

¼ cup plain yogurt (not nonfat or "light")

¼ cup sugar, optional

1 tablespoon vanilla extract, optional

ACCESSORIES

Thermometer

Just the Basics

Instant Pot sells extra rubber seals for the inside of the lid. It's a good idea to have a dedicated rubber seal for delicately flavored recipes like this one, as the seals tend to absorb and transfer strong flavors like garlic or herbs.

YOGURT | 8 HOURS + BOIL PROCESS

1 Pour milk into the Instant Pot insert, lock lid, and seal pressure release vent.

2 Set Instant Pot to YOGURT, choosing the option twice, until the screen says BOIL.

3 The milk will slowly heat up to a boil, the Instant Pot will beep, and the screen will read YOGT. This could take over 30 minutes.

4 Remove lid, stir, and use a thermometer to check the temperature of the milk. It must be 180°F or above. If it is below that temperature, secure lid, set to SLOW COOK on LOW, and let cook 10 minutes before checking the temperature again.

5 Remove insert from the cooker and let milk cool until it is 110°F. This will take around 1 hour at room temperature but can be sped up by placing the insert in a baking dish filled with ice and stirring the milk to keep it moving.

6 Once cooled, skim any skin off the top of the milk and discard. Transfer 1 cup of the cooked milk to a mixing bowl and whisk in plain yogurt. Then, whisk this yogurt mixture into the full insert of milk.

7 For plain yogurt, skip this step. For sweetened vanilla yogurt, whisk in sugar and vanilla extract.

8 Place the insert back into the Instant Pot, secure lid, and set to YOGURT for 8 hours. You do not need to seal the pressure valve for this step.

9 After cooking, cover and refrigerate at least 4 hours before serving.

Notes

Soups and Stews

pressure cook

Caitlin's Beef Stew and Dumplings

This is a great Sunday dinner recipe from my mother, which has now become one of my daughter Caitlin's favorite dishes to make in her Instant Pot. We made a few changes to simplify my mom's recipe (especially using canned biscuit dough in place of homemade dumplings), but the spirit and flavors of my mom's dish are all here!

Ingredients

2 pounds beef stew meat

Salt and pepper

$1/2$ cup all-purpose flour

3 tablespoons vegetable oil, divided

4 cups beef stock

2 tablespoons minced garlic

1 tablespoon sugar

2 bay leaves

$1/2$ teaspoon dried thyme

2 large carrots, coarsely chopped

2 stalks celery, coarsely chopped

2 potatoes, coarsely chopped

1 white onion, coarsely chopped

1 cup frozen peas

3 tablespoons cornstarch

$1/4$ cup water

1 (5-count) can Grands biscuits

Just the Basics

> My mother would add $1/4$ cup of chopped leeks to the broth along with the garlic for a great onion flavor. I've only omitted it here to make things a little simpler to shop for and prepare.

MEAT/STEW | HIGH PRESSURE | 30 MINUTES | QUICK RELEASE

1. Generously season stew meat with salt and pepper and toss in flour to coat. Preheat the Instant Pot insert on SAUTÉ. Add 1 tablespoon of the vegetable oil and heat until it thins out.

2. Add the floured stew meat in 2 to 3 batches to the insert and brown, adding additional oil for each batch and removing batches to a plate.

3. Pour in beef stock and deglaze the insert before stirring in all browned stew meat, garlic, sugar, bay leaves, and thyme.

4. Secure lid and seal pressure release vent. Set Instant Pot to MEAT/STEW on HIGH pressure for 25 minutes.

5. Once cook time has elapsed, carefully perform a QUICK RELEASE of the pressure.

6. Stir in carrots, celery, potatoes, and onion. Secure lid and seal pressure release vent. Set Instant Pot to MEAT/STEW on HIGH pressure for 5 minutes.

7. Once cook time has elapsed, carefully perform a QUICK RELEASE of the pressure.

8. Set Instant Pot to SAUTÉ, stir in peas, and bring up to a simmer. Whisk cornstarch into $1/4$ cup of water and stir into the cooking liquid, cooking 1 minute or until thickened. Season with salt and pepper to taste.

9. Cut each raw biscuit into 4 pieces and drop into the stew. Press down to lightly cover with broth. Cover with a glass lid and let cook 10 minutes, flipping dumplings occasionally, just until dumplings are cooked throughout.

Notes

Vegetable Stock

As far as store-bought stock goes, I find that vegetable stock has the least flavor and can really vary from brand to brand. Making it homemade will also deliver results that vary from batch to batch, depending on the extra scraps I throw in, but each batch is always delicious!

Ingredients

1 tablespoon olive oil

4 ounces baby bella
mushrooms, halved

1 yellow onion,
unpeeled, quartered

10 cups water

2 large carrots, chopped

2 large stalks celery, chopped

2 teaspoons minced garlic

2 bay leaves

1 teaspoon whole peppercorns

1 teaspoon salt

SOUP/BROTH | HIGH PRESSURE | 30 MINUTES | NATURAL RELEASE

1 Preheat the Instant Pot insert on SAUTÉ. Add olive oil and heat until it thins out.

2 Add mushrooms and onion and let cook, without stirring, until the mushrooms begin to brown on the bottom.

3 Pour in some of the water and deglaze the insert before stirring in carrots, celery, garlic, bay leaves, peppercorns, and salt.

4 Fill with enough water to reach the MAX FILL line.

5 Secure lid and seal pressure release vent.

6 Set Instant Pot to SOUP/BROTH on HIGH pressure for 30 minutes.

7 Once cook time has elapsed, let the pressure release through NATURAL RELEASE.

8 Discard vegetables. Let cool 30 minutes.

9 Strain the broth through a fine mesh strainer. Cover and refrigerate until ready to use.

Make it My Way

I will often make stock with vegetable scraps and a mixture of fresh herbs (thyme, sage, and/or rosemary). It doesn't have to be an exact science! I will even throw in leftover cooked vegetables from time to time. Roasted vegetables are especially good for making stock.

Just the Basics

You should always wash vegetables before using, but there's no need to peel or trim any of the vegetables in this stock.

Notes

SOUPS

Chicken Stock

As you will always need a bit of liquid to cook under pressure, stocks are invaluable. Whether it is a soup, rice, or even vegetable dish, using homemade chicken stock in place of water will add depth and flavor. Whenever we have a whole chicken for dinner, I always save the scraps to make a batch of stock that I will then use to make my next few meals.

Ingredients

Bones and scraps from
  1 whole chicken

1 yellow onion, quartered

1 carrot, chopped

2 stalks celery, chopped

2 sprigs fresh thyme

2 bay leaves

1 teaspoon salt

1 teaspoon whole peppercorns

SOUP/BROTH | HIGH PRESSURE | 1 HOUR | NATURAL RELEASE

1 Place all ingredients in the Instant Pot insert and then fill with enough water to reach the MAX FILL line.

2 Secure lid and seal pressure release vent.

3 Set Instant Pot to SOUP/BROTH on HIGH pressure for 1 hour.

4 Once cook time has elapsed, let the pressure release through NATURAL RELEASE.

5 Discard bones, scraps, and vegetables. Let cool 30 minutes.

6 Strain the broth through a fine mesh strainer.

7 Cover and refrigerate until ready to use. Use a spoon to skim the solidified fats off the top of the stock before using.

Make it My Way

I will often make stock with vegetable scraps and a mixture of fresh herbs (thyme, sage, and/or rosemary). The best part is that YOU get to choose what is added!

Just the Basics

This is particularly good when made from rotisserie chicken bones and scraps, as the roasted flavor adds another dimension to the stock.

Notes

Chili

Chili is a perfect Instant Pot dish, as a truly great chili is all about the melding and infusing of flavors—something that pressure cooking simply excels at. Just be sure to serve it with your favorite toppings!

Ingredients

1 tablespoon vegetable oil

1½ pounds ground beef

1 yellow onion, chopped

1 green bell pepper, chopped

1 jalapeño pepper,
  seeded and diced

1½ tablespoons chili powder

1 tablespoon minced garlic

1½ teaspoons ground cumin

½ cup beef stock

1 (28-ounce) can diced
  tomatoes (with liquid)

1 (15.5-ounce) can dark red
  kidney beans, drained

¼ cup chopped fresh cilantro

¾ teaspoon salt

½ teaspoon pepper

3 tablespoons tomato paste

SOUP/BROTH | HIGH PRESSURE | 12 MINUTES | NATURAL RELEASE

1 Preheat the Instant Pot insert on SAUTÉ. Add vegetable oil and heat until it thins out.

2 Add ground beef and cook until browned. Drain well.

3 Add onion, bell pepper, jalapeño, chili powder, garlic, and cumin and sauté for 3 minutes, just until onion begins to turn translucent.

4 Pour in beef stock and deglaze the insert before stirring in diced tomatoes, kidney beans, cilantro, salt, and pepper.

5 Spoon the tomato paste atop the chili, but do not stir in.

6 Secure lid and seal pressure release vent.

7 Set Instant Pot to SOUP/BROTH on HIGH pressure for 12 minutes.

8 Once cook time has elapsed, let the pressure release through NATURAL RELEASE. Stir chili well before serving.

Make it My Way

For a milder, less acidic, and somewhat sweeter chili, stir in ½ teaspoon of baking soda after cooking. The baking soda will neutralize the acid of the tomatoes, leaving behind their flavor and sweetness without their bite.

Just the Basics

Leaving the tomato paste atop the other liquid in the cooker allows it to cook without thickening the chili and risking the chance of the natural sugars in the tomatoes burning onto the bottom of the pot.

Notes _____

_____

SOUPS

Potsticker Wonton Soup

Frozen potstickers make for the easiest wonton dumplings in this delicious re-creation of a Chinese takeout favorite. I like to add shredded carrots and sliced mushrooms, which you don't normally find at restaurants, just to fill the soup out even more.

Ingredients

8 cups chicken stock

2 tablespoons soy sauce

1 tablespoon sesame oil

¼ teaspoon onion powder

¼ teaspoon white pepper

16 frozen pork potstickers
(about 16 ounces)

⅔ cup shredded carrots

4 button mushrooms, thinly sliced

⅓ cup chopped scallions

1 tablespoon cornstarch, optional

2 tablespoons water, optional

SOUP/BROTH | LOW PRESSURE | 1 MINUTE | QUICK RELEASE

1 Pour chicken stock into the Instant Pot insert and stir in soy sauce, sesame oil, onion powder, and white pepper. Drop in frozen potstickers.

2 Secure lid and seal pressure release vent.

3 Set Instant Pot to SOUP/BROTH on LOW pressure for 1 minute.

4 Once cook time has elapsed, carefully perform a QUICK RELEASE of the pressure.

5 Stir in carrots, mushrooms, and scallions and let stand 3 minutes to lightly cook the vegetables before serving.

6 For a slightly thicker broth that is closer to true takeout soup, as soon as you add the vegetables, switch the Instant Pot to SAUTÉ and bring up to a simmer. Whisk cornstarch into 2 tablespoons of water and then stir into the simmering broth, letting cook 1 minute.

Make it My Way

Any frozen potstickers will work in this soup, but I like to make it with 24 of The Perfect Gourmet Mini Potstickers that I order off of QVC. The mini potstickers make for a more spoon-friendly soup!

Just the Basics

While the pork potstickers are closer to a true Wonton Soup, many stores also sell frozen chicken potstickers if you would prefer to use chicken. Vegetable stock and vegetarian potstickers also can be used to make this fully vegetarian.

Notes _____

_____

45

SOUPS

Loaded Potato Chowder

This potato chowder is cooked with bacon and topped with Cheddar cheese and chives, just like a loaded baked potato. But there is one secret ingredient that really makes this recipe special: instant mashed potato flakes! The potato flakes are stirred in after cooking to add more potato flavor and thicken the chowder with no additional cooking steps.

Ingredients

5 slices bacon, diced

1 small yellow onion, chopped

¾ cup diced celery

2 teaspoons minced garlic

5 cups chicken stock

5 medium potatoes, peeled and chopped

1 small bay leaf

1 teaspoon salt

½ teaspoon pepper

½ teaspoon onion powder

1 cup heavy cream

Instant mashed potato flakes

Shredded sharp Cheddar cheese, to top

Chopped chives, to top

SOUP/BROTH | HIGH PRESSURE | 7 MINUTES | NATURAL RELEASE

1 Preheat the Instant Pot insert on SAUTÉ.

2 Place bacon, onion, celery, and garlic in the insert and sauté until bacon is nearly crisp.

3 Pour in chicken stock and deglaze the insert before stirring in potatoes, bay leaf, salt, pepper, and onion powder.

4 Secure lid and seal pressure release vent.

5 Set Instant Pot to SOUP/BROTH on HIGH pressure for 7 minutes.

6 Once cook time has elapsed, let the pressure release through NATURAL RELEASE for 10 minutes before quick releasing any remaining pressure.

7 Stir in heavy cream and then gradually stir in instant potato flakes a few tablespoons at a time until the soup has reached the desired thickness.

8 Adjust seasoning with additional salt and pepper to taste before serving topped with Cheddar cheese and chives.

Just the Basics

Be sure to stir for around 30 seconds each time you add more instant potato flakes, as they thicken more as they stand. If you've over-thickened, simply add additional heavy cream, milk, or water.

Notes

Homemade Chicken Noodle Soup

This soup is truly made from scratch—starting from a whole chicken—in only a little over an hour from prep to table. While it may be a little more prep work than other recipes in this book, you truly can't beat a fully homemade soup.

Ingredients

2 tablespoons olive oil

1 large yellow onion, chopped

1 cup chopped celery

2 medium carrots, chopped

3 tablespoons minced garlic

7 cups water, divided

1 bay leaf

1½ teaspoons salt

½ teaspoon pepper

½ teaspoon dried rosemary

½ teaspoon dried thyme

1 (3-pound) whole (raw) chicken, rinsed

8 ounces wide egg noodles

¼ cup chopped fresh parsley

SOUP/BROTH | HIGH PRESSURE | 25 MINUTES | NATURAL RELEASE

1 Preheat the Instant Pot insert on SAUTÉ. Add olive oil and heat until it thins out. Add onion, celery, carrots, and garlic, and sauté for 3 minutes, just until onion begins to turn translucent.

2 Pour in 1 cup of the water and deglaze the insert before stirring in bay leaf, salt, pepper, rosemary, and thyme.

3 Place the chicken breast side up in the pot. Pour in remaining 6 cups of water or as much of that water as you can add before getting to the MAX FILL line.

4 Secure lid and seal pressure release vent.

5 Set Instant Pot to SOUP/BROTH on HIGH pressure for 25 minutes.

6 Once cook time has elapsed, let the pressure release through NATURAL RELEASE for 15 minutes before quick releasing any remaining pressure.

7 Using tongs, carefully remove the whole chicken and transfer to a baking dish or large bowl.

8 Skim excess fat off the top of the broth and discard. Set Instant Pot to SAUTÉ and bring the broth up to a simmer. Stir in egg noodles and cook 7 minutes or just until tender.

9 As the noodles cook, pull the chicken meat from the whole chicken and chop any large pieces. Discard chicken skin. Stir the chopped chicken back into the soup and adjust seasoning with additional salt and pepper to taste before serving topped with fresh parsley.

Just the Basics

This can easily be made gluten free by preparing with gluten-free pasta of any shape or size.

Notes

Broccoli Cheddar Soup

This Broccoli Cheddar Soup tastes just like the kind you'd get at that famous "bread company" and sandwich shop. It's an absolute classic, made with very minimal prep and only 1 minute under pressure!

Ingredients

4 cups chicken stock

1 bunch broccoli, chopped (about 4 cups)

1 cup shredded carrots

3 tablespoons minced yellow onion

1 tablespoon cornstarch

1¼ cups milk

8 ounces processed cheese (such as Velveeta), chopped

1¼ cups shredded sharp Cheddar cheese

Salt and pepper to taste

SOUP/BROTH | LOW PRESSURE | 1 MINUTE | QUICK RELEASE

1 Pour chicken stock into the Instant Pot insert and stir in broccoli, carrots, and onion.

2 Secure lid and seal pressure release vent.

3 Set Instant Pot to SOUP/BROTH on LOW pressure for 1 minute.

4 Once cook time has elapsed, carefully perform a QUICK RELEASE of the pressure.

5 Set Instant Pot to SAUTÉ.

6 Whisk cornstarch into milk and stir into the soup. Bring up to a simmer and, stirring constantly, let cook 1 minute.

7 Turn off cooker and stir in processed cheese and Cheddar cheese until melted throughout. Season with salt and pepper to taste before serving.

Just the Basics

The processed cheese is what gives this soup such a smooth texture, while the Cheddar gives it a robust flavor. If you prefer, you can prepare it with less processed ingredients by increasing the cornstarch to 1½ tablespoons and increasing the Cheddar to 2 cups. It will not be as smooth, but the flavors will still be great.

Notes

Chicken and Rice Soup

While my Homemade Chicken Noodle Soup (recipe page 47) is made from a whole chicken, my recipe for this other classic chicken soup requires a lot less prep work thanks to starting with boneless chicken thighs.

Ingredients

1 tablespoon olive oil

1 tablespoon butter

1 pound boneless, skinless chicken thighs, chopped

1 small yellow onion, chopped

2 carrots, chopped

2 stalks celery, chopped

2 teaspoons minced garlic

4 cups chicken stock

1 (14.5-ounce) can diced tomatoes, with liquid

$\frac{1}{2}$ cup long grain white rice

2 sprigs fresh thyme

1 bay leaf

$\frac{1}{2}$ teaspoon salt

$\frac{1}{4}$ teaspoon pepper

SOUP/BROTH | HIGH PRESSURE | 4 MINUTES | NATURAL RELEASE

1 Preheat the Instant Pot insert on SAUTÉ. Add olive oil and butter and heat until sizzling.

2 Add chicken and sauté 3 minutes before adding onion, carrots, celery, and garlic. Sauté an additional 4 minutes or until vegetables begin to soften.

3 Pour in chicken stock and deglaze the insert before stirring in diced tomatoes, rice, thyme, bay leaf, salt, and pepper.

4 Secure lid and seal pressure release vent.

5 Set Instant Pot to SOUP/BROTH on HIGH pressure for 4 minutes.

6 Once cook time has elapsed, let the pressure release through NATURAL RELEASE for 10 minutes before quick releasing any remaining pressure.

7 Adjust salt and pepper to taste before serving.

Make it My Way

For a creamy broth, stir in $\frac{1}{2}$ cup of heavy cream after cooking.

Just the Basics

This can be made with boneless, skinless chicken breasts in place of the thighs, but I find that the thighs come out more tender.

Notes

Creamy Tomato Soup

The Instant Pot develops a ton of flavors in this tomato soup in only 7 minutes of cooking under pressure. For the full experience, you simply must serve this with a grilled cheese sandwich for dipping!

Ingredients

1 tablespoon olive oil

1 tablespoon butter

1 small yellow onion, diced

2 carrots, diced

2 cups vegetable stock

1 (28-ounce) can crushed tomatoes

2 teaspoons sugar

1/2 teaspoon Italian seasoning

1/4 teaspoon onion powder

1/4 teaspoon garlic powder

1/4 cup heavy cream

3 tablespoons chopped fresh basil

Salt and pepper to taste

SOUP/BROTH | HIGH PRESSURE | 7 MINUTES | NATURAL RELEASE

1. Preheat the Instant Pot insert on SAUTÉ. Add olive oil and butter and heat until sizzling.

2. Add onion and carrots and sauté for 5 minutes, just until onion softens.

3. Pour in vegetable stock and deglaze the insert before stirring in crushed tomatoes, sugar, Italian seasoning, onion powder, and garlic powder.

4. Secure lid and seal pressure release vent.

5. Set Instant Pot to SOUP/BROTH on HIGH pressure for 7 minutes.

6. Once cook time has elapsed, let the pressure release through NATURAL RELEASE for 10 minutes before quick releasing any remaining pressure.

7. For the best texture, fully blend the soup using an immersion blender or by transferring to a standard blender in batches.

8. Stir in heavy cream and basil before seasoning with salt and pepper to taste.

Make it My Way

I like to top this with shredded or shaved Parmesan cheese.

Just the Basics

For an even thicker soup, you can bring it up to a simmer after blending and adding the heavy cream, and let simmer, stirring constantly, for 5 minutes, just until slightly thickened.

Notes

SOUPS

Black Bean Soup

One of the greatest strengths of the Instant Pot is that you can cook dried beans in a fraction of the time of other methods and without any need to presoak them overnight. It allows you to make a luxurious soup like this one any day of the week.

Ingredients

1 tablespoon olive oil

1 red onion, chopped

1 tablespoon minced garlic

1 tablespoon chili powder

1 teaspoon ground cumin

4 cups vegetable stock

1 pound dried black beans, sorted and rinsed

1½ cups water

⅓ cup chopped fresh cilantro

1 bay leaf

1 tablespoon sugar

1 teaspoon onion powder

Juice of 1 small lime

Salt and pepper to taste

BEAN/GRAIN | HIGH PRESSURE | 30 MINUTES | NATURAL RELEASE

1 Preheat the Instant Pot insert on SAUTÉ. Add olive oil and heat until it thins out.

2 Add onion, garlic, chili powder, and cumin and sauté for 3 minutes, just until onion begins to turn translucent.

3 Pour in vegetable stock and deglaze the insert before stirring in beans, water, cilantro, bay leaf, sugar, and onion powder.

4 Secure lid and seal pressure release vent.

5 Set Instant Pot to BEAN/GRAIN or PRESSURE COOK on HIGH pressure for 30 minutes.

6 Once cook time has elapsed, let the pressure release through NATURAL RELEASE.

7 For the best texture, purée about half of the beans. This is easiest when done with an immersion blender, but you also can transfer half of the soup to a blender or food processor to purée before stirring back into the rest of the soup.

8 Stir in lime juice and season generously with salt and pepper to taste before serving.

Make it My Way

I like to top this with fresh pico de gallo and a drizzle of sour cream thinned out with milk.

Just the Basics

For an even thicker soup, you can bring it up to a simmer after cooking and stir in 1 tablespoon of cornstarch whisked into 2 tablespoons of water.

Notes

SOUPS

Pasta Fagioli Soup

You'll find out throughout this book that I absolutely love pasta! This simple soup takes ditalini pasta (small and short tubes) and cooks them directly in a tomato and vegetable stock that is full of Italian flavors.

Ingredients

2 tablespoons olive oil

1 small red onion, diced

2 stalks celery, diced

2 carrots, diced

1 tablespoon minced garlic

1 teaspoon Italian seasoning

¼ teaspoon crushed red pepper flakes

5 cups vegetable stock

1 (24-ounce) pasta sauce

1 (15-ounce) can cannellini beans, drained

8 ounces ditalini pasta

¼ cup chopped fresh basil

Salt and pepper to taste

PRESSURE COOK | HIGH PRESSURE | 4 MINUTES | QUICK RELEASE

1 Preheat the Instant Pot insert on SAUTÉ. Add olive oil and heat until it thins out.

2 Add onion, celery, carrots, garlic, Italian seasoning, and red pepper flakes and sauté for 4 minutes, just until onion begins to turn translucent.

3 Pour in vegetable stock and deglaze the insert before stirring in pasta sauce, beans, and pasta.

4 Secure lid and seal pressure release vent.

5 Set Instant Pot to PRESSURE COOK on HIGH pressure for 4 minutes.

6 Once cook time has elapsed, carefully perform a QUICK RELEASE of the pressure.

7 Stir in basil and season with salt and pepper to taste before serving.

Make it My Way

I like to serve this topped with shredded Parmesan cheese and alongside crusty Italian bread. I also like to include browned hamburger meat, as this was Lois, my mother-in-law's, favorite soup! She thought it tasted better than the Pasta Fagioli Soup from the Italian restaurant that I used to manage!

Just the Basics

While this is vegetarian, many versions of Pasta Fagioli have meat in them. Chopped bacon is particularly good as long as you brown it and drain excess grease before cooking the soup under pressure.

Notes _____

Split Pea and Ham Soup

Split pea soup is often overlooked because of how long it takes to prepare using traditional methods, but this recipe shows that it can be made from dried peas in only 15 minutes under pressure! Cooking it with a whole ham hock brings a ton of flavor and a surprising amount of meat that you can shred into the soup after cooking.

Ingredients

1 tablespoon vegetable oil

1 small yellow onion, diced

2 stalks celery, diced

2 carrots, diced

2 teaspoons minced garlic

6 cups chicken stock

1 pound dried split peas, rinsed

1 whole ham hock, or
1 chopped ham steak

2 bay leaves

1 tablespoon sugar

3/4 teaspoon salt

1/2 teaspoon pepper

BEAN/GRAIN | HIGH PRESSURE | 15 MINUTES | NATURAL RELEASE

1 Preheat the Instant Pot insert on SAUTÉ. Add vegetable oil and heat until it thins out.

2 Add onion, celery, carrots, and garlic and sauté for 4 minutes, just until onion begins to turn translucent.

3 Pour in chicken stock and deglaze the insert before stirring in peas, ham hock, bay leaves, sugar, salt, and pepper.

4 Secure lid and seal pressure release vent.

5 Set Instant Pot to BEAN/GRAIN or PRESSURE COOK on HIGH pressure for 15 minutes.

6 Once cook time has elapsed, let the pressure release through NATURAL RELEASE.

7 Remove meat from the ham hock and discard bone before serving.

Make it My Way

The ham hock bone adds a lot of flavor to this soup, so if you use a ham steak, a bone-in ham steak is best. You can chop the meat and add along with the bone. Just be sure to discard the bone before serving!

Just the Basics

The small amount of sugar in this really brightens up the peas, replicating the natural sugars found in fresh peas.

Notes

Sausage and Tortellini Soup

This hearty soup has cheese-filled tortellini and crumbled Italian sausage in a rich and creamy tomato sauce. While it only takes 2 minutes under pressure, it truly tastes like it has been building flavors all day long.

Ingredients

1 tablespoon olive oil

1 pound ground Italian sausage

1 cup chopped carrots

3/4 cup diced red onion

1 tablespoon minced garlic

1 teaspoon dry rubbed sage

1/4 teaspoon crushed red pepper flakes

5 cups vegetable stock

1 1/2 cups prepared pasta sauce

1 (12-ounce) bag dried tortellini

2 cups frozen chopped spinach

3/4 cup heavy cream

Salt and pepper to taste

SOUP/BROTH | HIGH PRESSURE | 2 MINUTES | QUICK RELEASE

1 Preheat the Instant Pot insert on SAUTÉ. Add olive oil and heat until it thins out.

2 Add ground sausage and cook until browned. Drain well.

3 Add carrots, onion, garlic, sage, and red pepper flakes and sauté for 3 minutes, just until onion begins to turn translucent.

4 Pour in vegetable stock and deglaze the insert before stirring in pasta sauce and tortellini.

5 Secure lid and seal pressure release vent.

6 Set Instant Pot to SOUP/BROTH on HIGH pressure for 2 minutes.

7 Once cook time has elapsed, carefully perform a QUICK RELEASE of the pressure.

8 Stir in chopped spinach and heavy cream before seasoning with salt and pepper to taste.

Make it My Way

The crushed red pepper flakes give this just a bit of heat but can be omitted, if desired. For even more heat, use hot Italian sausage.

Just the Basics

The tortellini used in this recipe is the kind that you will find in the ordinary dried pasta aisle. I use the plain cheese variety sold by Barilla.

Notes

Appetizers and Snacks

pressure cook

slow cook

Hawaiian Meatballs

This is my variation on a party staple of meatballs in a sweet and tangy barbecue-style sauce. I use sweet-and-sour sauce rather than the traditional chili sauce and add pineapple and red bell pepper for some Hawaiian flair.

Ingredients

¾ cup beef stock

½ cup barbecue sauce

1 tablespoon soy sauce

1 tablespoon sesame oil

32 ounces frozen meatballs

¾ cup sweet-and-sour sauce

1½ cups fresh or canned pineapple chunks

¼ cup diced red bell pepper

¼ cup chopped scallions

PRESSURE COOK | HIGH PRESSURE | 5 MINUTES | QUICK RELEASE

1 In the Instant Pot insert, stir to combine beef stock, barbecue sauce, soy sauce, and sesame oil. Place frozen meatballs over top but do not stir.

2 Secure lid and seal pressure release vent.

3 Set Instant Pot to PRESSURE COOK on HIGH pressure for 5 minutes.

4 Once cook time has elapsed, carefully perform a QUICK RELEASE of the pressure.

5 Stir in sweet-and-sour sauce before folding in pineapple, bell pepper, and scallions.

6 Serve immediately, or set Instant Pot to SLOW COOK on LOW to keep hot while entertaining.

Make it My Way

Any type of frozen meatballs will work in this recipe; however, I prefer ones that are not labeled as "Italian-style," as the Italian herbs don't go well with the ingredients in this dish.

Just the Basics

Sweet-and-sour sauce can usually be purchased in the Asian foods section of the grocery store. Duck sauce will also work. Teriyaki glaze is also quite good, but I would suggest omitting the soy sauce if using that, as there will already be a lot of sodium in anything "teriyaki."

Notes

Philly Steak Nachos

Cheesesteaks are a true Philly favorite, and these nachos take everything that makes them great and serve it up in a whole new way that is perfect for parties! So, skip the nacho cheese and go for that classic Philly Cheez Whiz!

Ingredients

- 2 tablespoons vegetable oil, divided
- 1 tablespoon butter
- 1 small yellow onion, sliced
- 1 small green bell pepper, sliced
- 8 ounces sliced button mushrooms
- Montreal steak seasoning
- 1 pound sirloin steak, thinly sliced
- 1/2 cup beef stock
- 1/2 teaspoon Worcestershire sauce
- 1/4 teaspoon onion powder
- 1 cup cheese sauce (such as Cheez Whiz)
- 12 ounces tortilla chips

MEAT/STEW | HIGH PRESSURE | 8 MINUTES | NATURAL RELEASE

1 Preheat the Instant Pot insert on SAUTÉ. Add 1 tablespoon of vegetable oil and butter and heat until sizzling.

2 Add the yellow onion, bell pepper, and mushrooms and generously season with Montreal steak seasoning. Sauté until all vegetables are tender, about 8 minutes. Remove and set aside.

3 Heat the remaining tablespoon of vegetable oil before adding steak and seasoning generously with Montreal steak seasoning. Brown steak on at least 1 side.

4 Pour in beef stock and deglaze the insert before stirring in Worcestershire sauce and onion powder.

5 Secure lid and seal pressure release vent.

6 Set Instant Pot to MEAT/STEW on HIGH pressure for 8 minutes.

7 Once cook time has elapsed, let the pressure release through NATURAL RELEASE for 5 minutes before quick releasing any remaining pressure. Stir the cooked vegetables into the cooking liquid to reheat them.

8 Meanwhile, microwave the cheese sauce in 30 second intervals, stirring each time, until hot.

9 Arrange tortilla chips on a large sheet pan or 2 small sheet pans. Drain the steak and vegetables well and disperse over the chips. Drizzle with the hot cheese sauce before serving.

Just the Basics

Cheez Whiz is very thick. I find that adding a few tablespoons of milk makes it much easier to drizzle over the nachos. You can use shredded cheese and place under the broiler to melt, but Cheez Whiz is the true Philly way!

Notes

Perfect Hard-Boiled Eggs

Making a perfect hard-boiled egg is made easy thanks to the Instant Pot and the "5-5-5 method." It takes 5 minutes of cooking under pressure, then 5 minutes of natural release, then 5 minutes in an ice bath to cool down. The truly great thing is that, when cooked under pressure, the eggs are usually far easier to peel than when you boil them on the stove.

Ingredients

Up to 18 large eggs

EGG | HIGH PRESSURE | 5 MINUTES | NATURAL RELEASE

1. Place a steam rack in Instant Pot insert and pour in 1 cup of water.

2. Carefully arrange the eggs over the steam rack, stacking them so that they will all fit.

3. Secure lid and seal pressure release vent.

4. Set Instant Pot to EGG or PRESSURE COOK on HIGH pressure for 5 minutes.

5. Once cook time has elapsed, let the pressure release through NATURAL RELEASE for 5 minutes before quick releasing any remaining pressure.

6. Using tongs, carefully transfer the cooked eggs to a large bowl of ice water. Let stand 5 minutes.

7. Peel and serve.

Make it My Way

You've got to use these eggs to make my Best Deviled Eggs recipe on the next page!

Just the Basics

Eggs that are closer to their expiration date will peel even easier than fresher eggs. Organic, brown, or truly farm-fresh eggs are notoriously hard to peel.

Notes

APPETIZERS

Best Deviled Eggs

I make my deviled eggs with a ton of celery flavor, rather than using the sweet relish found in many other recipes. It's a subtle change but one that has always made my deviled eggs a huge hit at family gatherings! I will often prepare them the night before so that they are nice and cold once the guests start arriving.

Ingredients

12 hard-boiled eggs

$2/3$ cup mayonnaise

1 stalk celery, minced

1 tablespoon yellow mustard

1 teaspoon sugar

$1/4$ teaspoon celery salt

$1/4$ teaspoon paprika

Salt, optional

Chopped parsley, for garnish

1 Peel eggs under cool running water and pat dry.

2 Slice eggs in half and scoop yolks into a mixing bowl. Arrange whites on a serving platter.

3 Using a heavy fork, mash mayonnaise, celery, mustard, sugar, celery salt, and paprika into the yolks until almost entirely smooth.

4 For the best flavor, lightly season the egg whites with salt before filling.

5 Transfer the yolk filling to a pastry bag or food storage bag with the corner cut off and pipe the filling into each egg white.

6 Garnish with chopped parsley and a sprinkling of additional paprika, if desired.

Make it My Way

I love to sprinkle the tops of these with Bacon Salt that I purchased off of QVC. Smoked paprika will also give you some of that smoky bacon flavor.

Just the Basics

The little bit of added sugar in this recipe replicates the sweet relish used in more traditional preparations, but most of the flavor is coming from celery instead.

Notes

APPETIZERS

(V)

Refried Bean Dip

Even though it starts from dried beans, not canned, this Southwestern party dip is much easier than you may think and far more flavorful than any store-bought bean dip.

Ingredients

1 pound dried pinto beans, sorted and rinsed

4 cups vegetable stock

1 cup water

1 red onion diced, divided

1 large jalapeño pepper, seeded and diced

1 packet taco seasoning mix

1 bay leaf

1 cup chunky salsa

1 cup shredded Mexican cheese blend

BEAN/GRAIN | HIGH PRESSURE | 45 MINUTES | NATURAL RELEASE

1 In the Instant Pot insert, stir together pinto beans, vegetable stock, water, $2/3$ of the diced red onion, jalapeño pepper, taco seasoning, and bay leaf.

2 Secure lid and seal pressure release vent.

3 Set Instant Pot to BEAN/GRAIN or PRESSURE COOK on HIGH pressure for 45 minutes.

4 Once cook time has elapsed, let the pressure release through NATURAL RELEASE. Drain and reserve excess cooking liquid.

5 For a chunkier texture, use a potato masher to mash the cooked beans. For a smooth texture, transfer in batches to a food processor or blender and blend until smooth. Add a little bit of the reserved cooking liquid at a time, just until your desired texture has been reached.

6 Set Instant Pot to SLOW COOK on LESS for 30 minutes.

7 Stir in salsa and the remaining $1/3$ of the diced red onion before topping with the shredded cheese.

8 Cover with a glass lid and cook without stirring. Once cook time has elapsed, set to KEEP WARM and serve directly out of the pot.

APPETIZERS

Just the Basics

Always rinse and sort through dried beans to discard any irregularly shaped beans, as those may actually be small stones.

Notes

Infused Italian Pasta Salad

By cooking the pasta directly in the Italian dressing, this pasta salad is packed with flavor in a way that you simply cannot achieve any other way.

Ingredients

1 (12-ounce) box tri-colored rotini

2 ½ cups water

1 cup zesty Italian salad dressing

2 teaspoons minced garlic

½ teaspoon Italian seasoning

½ cup ice water

¼ cup ice

1 (6-ounce dry weight) can whole black olives

8 ounces mozzarella cheese pearls

1 cup grape tomatoes, halved

3 tablespoons grated Parmesan cheese

2 tablespoons minced red onion

Salt and pepper to taste

PRESSURE COOK | HIGH PRESSURE | 5 MINUTES | QUICK RELEASE

1 Place rotini in the Instant Pot insert and stir in the 2 ½ cups water, salad dressing, garlic, and Italian seasoning.

2 Secure lid and seal pressure release vent.

3 Set Instant Pot to PRESSURE COOK on HIGH pressure for 5 minutes.

4 Once cook time has elapsed, carefully perform a QUICK RELEASE of the pressure.

5 Immediately stir in ice water and ice to cool the pasta down. No need to drain.

6 Fold in black olives, mozzarella cheese, grape tomatoes, Parmesan cheese, and red onion before seasoning with salt and pepper to taste.

7 Cover and refrigerate at least 1 hour before serving.

Make it My Way

This is the perfect dish to use my Rapid Slicer! It perfectly slices all of the olives and grape tomatoes evenly, and in seconds, cutting down the prep time!

Just the Basics

Carefully removing the insert from the Instant Pot after cooking will also help the pasta cool down before adding the other ingredients.

Notes _____

APPETIZERS

Honey Barbecue Chicken Wings

The Instant Pot makes cooking frozen chicken wings a breeze, while ensuring that they always come out tender and moist. After tossing them in a honey barbecue sauce, I throw them under the broiler just to give a quick crispness to the skin.

Ingredients

2 pounds frozen chicken wings

1¼ cups barbecue sauce

2 tablespoons honey

ACCESSORIES

Steam basket

STEAM | HIGH PRESSURE | 17 MINUTES | NATURAL RELEASE

1 Pour 1 cup of water into the Instant Pot insert and then lower steam basket into the pot.

2 Place the chicken wings in the steam basket.

3 In a large mixing bowl, whisk together barbecue sauce and honey. Drizzle ¼ cup of this mixture over the chicken wings and reserve the remainder until after cooking.

4 Secure lid and seal pressure release vent.

5 Set Instant Pot to STEAM on HIGH pressure for 17 minutes.

6 Once cook time has elapsed, let the pressure release naturally for 10 minutes before quick releasing any remaining pressure.

7 Drain wings and transfer to the barbecue sauce in the mixing bowl, tossing to coat. Place on a sheet pan lined with aluminum foil.

8 Place oven rack in the second position from the top and set broiler to HIGH.

9 Broil chicken wings until they begin to brown, about 4 minutes. For best flavor, flip and broil on the opposite side before serving.

Make it My Way

This also can be made with fresh wings by reducing the cook time from 17 minutes to 12 minutes. I typically like to use frozen, as they come pre-split into wing and drum sections, making prep a breeze.

Just the Basics

Instant Pot's new Air Fryer Lid can be used to brown the wings before serving. Simply lock lid in place and set to BROIL for 4 minutes on each side.

Notes _____

APPETIZERS

Crab-Boiled Peanuts

Ⓥ

Don't let the name fool you; there is no actual seafood in this Northern take on a Southern specialty. These tender boiled peanuts are simply cooked in a broth of Old Bay seasoning to give them all the flavors of a crab boil without any crab.

Ingredients

1 pound dried raw
   peanuts in the shell

¼ cup Old Bay seasoning

1 tablespoon dried parsley flakes

1 tablespoon salt

2 teaspoons hot pepper sauce

2 teaspoons vegetable oil

1 bay leaf

BEAN/GRAIN | HIGH PRESSURE | 60 MINUTES | NATURAL RELEASE

1 Place all ingredients in the Instant Pot insert and add just enough water to cover the peanuts entirely without hitting the MAX FILL line. Stir to disperse the spices.

2 Place a heavy ceramic plate over the peanuts to keep them from floating above the water.

3 Secure lid and seal pressure release vent.

4 Set Instant Pot to BEAN/GRAIN or PRESSURE COOK on HIGH pressure for 60 minutes.

5 Once cook time has elapsed, let the pressure release through NATURAL RELEASE.

6 Serve warm and store refrigerated in the cooking liquid.

Make it My Way

For even more flavor, use vegetable stock as some of the cooking liquid by adding 4 cups to the insert and then filling with water until the peanuts are submerged.

Just the Basics

The small amount of vegetable oil in this recipe is added to prevent the peanuts from building up foam as they cook.

Notes

APPETIZERS

Chili Queso

Queso is a party staple, especially when kept warm right inside a cooker like the Instant Pot. I like to make mine a little different, using canned chili in place of salsa or canned (Rotel) tomatoes.

Ingredients

12 ounces cream cheese, chopped

1 (15-ounce) can chili (may use vegetarian)

2 cups shredded Cheddar cheese

$3/4$ cup milk

$1/4$ cup chopped fresh cilantro

Salt and pepper to taste

SLOW COOK | LESS | 2 HOURS

1 Place cream cheese, chili, Cheddar cheese, milk, and cilantro in the Instant Pot insert and lightly mix.

2 Cover with a glass lid and set Instant Pot to SLOW COOK on LESS for 2 hours, stirring every 30 minutes. Stir well after cooking.

3 To serve at a party, set Instant Pot to KEEP WARM after cooking and stir every 30 minutes. If it cools down too much, simply switch to SLOW COOK on LESS.

Make it My Way

For the creamiest (but less homemade) queso, you can substitute 16 ounces of processed cheese (Velveeta) in place of all of the cream cheese, $1/4$ cup of the milk, and 1 cup of the Cheddar cheese.

Just the Basics

Any type of canned chili will work in this dip, but it's especially good when made using chili without beans. Or make it vegetarian by simply using a can of vegetarian chili.

Notes _____

Spinach and Artichoke Dip

This classic creamy dip is a great use of the Instant Pot's "slow cook" setting, as it is too thick and contains too much dairy to cook under pressure. The other plus is that you can keep it warm right inside the pot for serving at extended parties.

Ingredients

16 ounces cream cheese, softened

8 ounces sour cream

3/4 cup shredded Italian cheese blend

1/2 cup grated Parmesan cheese

1/3 cup milk

1 tablespoon sugar

3/4 teaspoon salt

1/2 teaspoon pepper

1/4 teaspoon Worcestershire sauce

1 1/2 cups frozen chopped spinach, thawed

1 (14-ounce) can artichoke hearts, drained and chopped

3 tablespoons minced red onion

1 tablespoon minced garlic

SLOW COOK | LESS | 2 HOURS

1 In a food processor, combine cream cheese, sour cream, Italian cheese, Parmesan cheese, milk, sugar, salt, pepper, and Worcestershire sauce and process until mostly smooth.

2 Transfer the cheese mixture to the Instant Pot insert and fold in spinach, artichoke hearts, red onion, and garlic.

3 Cover with a glass lid and set Instant Pot to SLOW COOK on LESS for 2 hours, stirring halfway through cooking. Stir well after cooking.

4 To serve at a party, set Instant Pot to KEEP WARM after cooking and stir every 30 minutes. If it cools down too much, simply switch to SLOW COOK on LESS.

Just the Basics

This can be made gluten-free by simply omitting the Worcestershire sauce.

Notes

Pepper Jam Cocktail Franks

It's hard to resist smoked cocktail franks in a sweet and savory sauce! It's one of those dishes you'll only ever get at a party, but one you keep walking back to all night long. For a slightly more grown-up take, I make these with pepper jam in place of the traditional grape jelly.

Ingredients

2 (16-ounce) packages cocktail franks

1¼ cups chili sauce

⅔ cup red or hot pepper jam

1 tablespoon Dijon mustard

½ teaspoon onion powder

SLOW COOK | LESS | 2 HOURS

1. Place all ingredients in the Instant Pot insert and stir to combine.

2. Cover with a glass lid and set Instant Pot to SLOW COOK on LESS for 2 hours, stirring halfway through cooking. Stir well after cooking.

3. To serve at a party, set Instant Pot to KEEP WARM after cooking and stir every 30 minutes. If it cools down too much, simply switch to SLOW COOK on LESS.

Make it My Way

I like to buy local pepper jams at the farmer's market whenever I can visit. Just be sure to taste them to gauge their spice level before adding. If the jam is especially spicy, I only add ⅓ of a cup.

Just the Basics

Chili sauce is similar to ketchup and usually is sold in the same aisle. In a pinch or when serving children, ½ cup of grape jelly can be used in place of the pepper jam for more traditional sweet and savory cocktail franks.

Notes

APPETIZERS

Heather's Buffalo Chicken Dip

This is my daughter Heather's go-to recipe. She makes this for all of our family holidays and get-togethers. Heather likes things a little spicy, so she'll sometimes add even more Buffalo sauce, but I love to make it just the way it is.

Ingredients

4 cups chopped cooked chicken

4 cups shredded Colby-Jack cheese

16 ounces cream cheese, softened

1 cup Buffalo wing sauce

1 cup ranch salad dressing

SLOW COOK | NORMAL | 2 HOURS

1 In the Instant Pot insert, fold together all ingredients until mostly combined.

2 Cover with a glass lid and set Instant Pot to SLOW COOK on NORMAL for 2 hours, stirring occasionally (I stir every 15 minutes just to be safe).

3 To serve at a party, set Instant Pot to KEEP WARM after cooking and stir every 30 minutes. If it cools down too much, simply switch to SLOW COOK on LESS.

Make it My Way

I use Frank's Red Hot brand Buffalo wing sauce to make this. It has a ton of flavor without being overwhelmingly spicy.

Just the Basics

This is great when made from a supermarket's cooked rotisserie chicken. One chicken will yield the right amount of meat for this recipe. In a pinch, you can use chopped Perdue Short Cuts or other precooked chicken.

Notes _____

Meats

pressure cook

Mom's Sunday Pot Roast with Gravy, 81

Barbecue Beef Brisket, 82

Shepherd's Pie, 83

Baby Back Ribs, 85

Swiss Steak, 86

Meat Loaf, 87

Pulled Pork, 89

 Apricot-Glazed Corned Beef, 90

Beef Burgundy, 91

Short Ribs with Plums, 93

Instant Pot Lasagna, 95

Pork Chops with Mushroom Gravy, 96

 Cuban Pork with Orange and Garlic, 97

Smoked Pork Chops with Warm Apple Slaw, 99

slow cook

 Bolognese Sauce, 100

sous vide

Hoisin-Glazed London Broil, 101

 Rosemary Pork Tenderloin, 103

Balsamic-Glazed Top Sirloin, 105

Mom's Sunday Pot Roast with Gravy

Having six children, my mom always was trying to find a way to stretch her dollar to feed all of us good, homemade meals. Buying less expensive cuts of meat to transform into delicious pot roast was the way she did that almost every Sunday. We always looked forward to Mom's Sunday Pot Roast!

Ingredients

1 tablespoon olive oil

1 (3-pound) beef chuck roast

Salt and pepper

1½ cups beef stock

1 tablespoon tomato paste

3 garlic cloves

2 bay leaves

6 medium red bliss potatoes, cut in half

3 medium carrots, peeled and chopped into 2-inch lengths

2–4 tablespoons all-purpose flour

¼ cup chopped fresh parsley

3 tablespoons butter, optional

Just the Basics

Deglazing the pot is a MUST, as any bits of meat stuck to the bottom could result in a "BURN" error message displaying on the Instant Pot screen. If this happens, QUICK RELEASE and thoroughly scrape the bottom before setting to the cook time that was remaining.

MEAT/STEW | HIGH PRESSURE | 75 MINUTES | QUICK RELEASE

1. Preheat the Instant Pot insert on SAUTÉ. Add olive oil. Generously season the roast with salt and pepper on all sides. Transfer to the Instant Pot and brown on all sides.

2. Remove roast and deglaze the insert with the beef stock before stirring in tomato paste, garlic, and bay leaves.

3. Return roast to the Instant Pot, secure lid, and seal pressure release vent.

4. Set Instant Pot to MEAT/STEW on HIGH pressure for 75 minutes.

5. Once cook time has elapsed, carefully perform a QUICK RELEASE of the pressure.

6. Add the potatoes and carrots over top of the roast, secure lid, and seal pressure release vent.

7. Set Instant Pot to PRESSURE COOK on HIGH pressure for 10 minutes.

8. Once cook time has elapsed, carefully perform a QUICK RELEASE of the pressure.

9. Discard bay leaves and transfer vegetables and roast to a serving platter, covering with aluminum foil as you prepare the gravy.

Preparing the Gravy

Set the Instant Pot to SAUTÉ and bring the cooking liquid up to a simmer. Whisk in flour a tablespoon at a time until your desired consistency is reached. For the smoothest gravy, strain through a mesh strainer. Season with salt and pepper to taste before serving over pot roast with plenty of chopped fresh parsley. For a richer gravy, stir in 3 tablespoons of butter after cooking.

MEATS

Notes

_____

_____

Barbecue Beef Brisket

Smokehouses will sometimes take an entire day to cook a tender beef brisket, but this recipe will have it on the table in less than 2 hours. It's a cut of meat that just wasn't very accessible to the home cook before the Instant Pot came along!

Ingredients

1 flat-cut beef brisket (about 3 pounds)

3 tablespoons vegetable oil, divided

2 tablespoons smoked paprika

2 teaspoons onion powder

2 teaspoons garlic powder

1 1/2 teaspoons salt

3/4 teaspoon pepper

3/4 teaspoon ground mustard

1 cup beef stock

3 tablespoons light brown sugar

3/4 cup barbecue sauce

1 1/2 tablespoons yellow mustard

MEAT/STEW | HIGH PRESSURE | 85 MINUTES | NATURAL RELEASE

1 Rub the brisket with 1 tablespoon of the vegetable oil. In a small bowl, combine smoked paprika, onion powder, garlic powder, salt, pepper, and ground mustard. Sprinkle the entire mixture over the brisket and rub into both sides.

2 Preheat the Instant Pot insert on SAUTÉ. Add the remaining 2 tablespoons of vegetable oil and heat until oil is thin and hot.

3 Add the brisket to the cooker and brown on both sides.

4 Remove brisket and deglaze the insert using beef stock.

5 Turn off cooker and place a steam rack over the beef stock in the insert. Place brisket on steam rack and top with brown sugar. Secure lid and seal pressure release vent.

6 Set Instant Pot to MEAT/STEW on HIGH pressure for 85 minutes.

7 Once cook time has elapsed, let the pressure release through NATURAL RELEASE.

8 Transfer brisket to a sheet pan. Whisk together barbecue sauce and yellow mustard and spread over the top of the brisket.

9 Place oven rack in the second position from the top and set to BROIL. Place brisket under the broiler and cook 3 to 4 minutes, just until the barbecue sauce is bubbly hot and beginning to brown.

Just the Basics

Instant Pot's new Air Fryer Lid also can be used to brown the barbecue sauce mixture. Lock the lid in place and set to BROIL for 3 minutes or until sauce is bubbly hot and beginning to brown.

Notes

Shepherd's Pie

Potatoes (for mashing) are steamed right above the meat filling to make all of the components of this Shepherd's Pie in one pot. Like most people in North America, I make my Shepherd's Pie with ground beef (which is technically called a "Cottage Pie"), but you could absolutely substitute ground lamb if you wanted something more authentic.

Ingredients

1 tablespoon vegetable oil

1 pound ground beef

1 small yellow onion, diced

2 carrots, diced

1 stalk celery, diced

2 tablespoons chopped fresh parsley

1½ cups beef stock

2 tablespoons tomato paste

1½ tablespoons Worcestershire sauce

4 medium Russet potatoes, peeled and chopped

¼ cup butter

2 tablespoons milk

Salt and pepper to taste

2 cups frozen peas

1½ tablespoons cornstarch

3 tablespoons water

ACCESSORIES

Steam basket

Just the Basics

Instant Pot's new Air Fryer Lid can be used to lightly brown the top of the potatoes before serving. Simply lock lid in place and set to BROIL for 4 minutes.

PRESSURE COOK | HIGH PRESSURE | 3 MINUTES | QUICK RELEASE

1 Preheat the Instant Pot insert on SAUTÉ. Add vegetable oil and heat until it thins out. Place ground beef in insert and sauté until browned. Drain excess grease before stirring in onion, carrots, celery, and parsley and sautéing 2 additional minutes.

2 Pour in beef stock and deglaze the insert before stirring in tomato paste and Worcestershire sauce.

3 Place chopped potatoes in a steam basket and lower into the insert over top of the ground beef and vegetables.

4 Secure lid and seal pressure release vent. Set Instant Pot to PRESSURE COOK on HIGH pressure for 3 minutes.

5 Once cook time has elapsed, carefully perform a QUICK RELEASE of the pressure.

6 Remove steam basket and transfer potatoes to a mixing bowl. Add butter and milk and, using a potato masher, mash until your desired consistency. Season with salt and pepper to taste.

7 Set Instant Pot to SAUTÉ and stir frozen peas into the ground beef and cooking liquid. Bring up to a simmer.

8 Whisk cornstarch into 3 tablespoons of water and stir into the simmering ground beef mixture. Let cook 1 minute or until thickened. Season with salt and pepper to taste.

9 Spoon mashed potatoes over top of the ground beef mixture, turn off cooker, cover with a glass lid, and let stand 3 minutes before serving.

Notes

Baby Back Ribs

Making truly tender ribs has always taken a ton of effort, but the Instant Pot cuts down on all that work immensely! While many people will bake (or even boil) their ribs for hours, it takes less than an hour under pressure to get even better results.

Ingredients

1 rack baby back ribs

1 tablespoon smoked paprika

2 teaspoons sugar

1 teaspoon salt

1/2 teaspoon pepper

1/2 teaspoon onion powder

1/4 teaspoon garlic powder

2 cups barbecue sauce, divided

MEAT/STEW | HIGH PRESSURE | 50 MINUTES | NATURAL RELEASE

1 Pour 1 cup of water into the Instant Pot insert and then place a steam rack over top.

2 Cut ribs into 3 or 4 sections that are small enough to fit into the Instant Pot insert.

3 In a small bowl, combine smoked paprika, sugar, salt, pepper, onion powder, and garlic powder to make a dry rub.

4 Cover the ribs in the dry rub and massage into the meat.

5 Brush ribs with 1 cup of the barbecue sauce before arranging inside the insert. Secure lid and seal pressure release vent.

6 Set Instant Pot to MEAT/STEW on HIGH pressure for 50 minutes.

7 Once cook time has elapsed, let the pressure release through NATURAL RELEASE for 10 minutes before quick releasing any remaining pressure.

8 Place cooked ribs on a sheet pan lined with aluminum foil and brush with the remaining barbecue sauce. Place oven rack in the second position from the top and set broiler to HIGH.

9 Broil ribs for 4 minutes or until barbecue sauce is bubbly hot and beginning to brown.

Make it My Way

I always love to use Corky's Original Bar-B-Q Sauce (keeping it in my QVC family), but you can use your own personal favorite!

Just the Basics

Whenever you cook ribs, you should remove the thin membrane on the underside to make them easier to eat. Simply slide a knife between the membrane and the bone to loosen it enough to pull it from the full rack.

MEATS

Notes ———————————

Swiss Steak

When I was growing up, my mother would always prepare this Swiss Steak on the stovetop, simmering it for hours. I made a few minor changes (thickening with cornstarch rather than flour) to faithfully adapt her recipe for the Instant Pot so I can make this personal favorite in a fraction of the time.

Ingredients

3 tablespoons vegetable oil, divided

8 ounces button mushrooms, halved

2 stalks celery, chopped

1 white onion, diced

1/2 green bell pepper, chopped

1 1/2 tablespoons minced garlic

2 pounds round or sirloin steak

Salt and pepper

1/2 cup beef stock

1 (14.5-ounce) can diced tomatoes, with liquid

2 teaspoons Worcestershire sauce

1 teaspoon sugar

1/2 teaspoon celery salt

1 tablespoon cornstarch

2 tablespoons water

Chopped fresh parsley, for garnish

MEAT/STEW | HIGH PRESSURE | 30 MINUTES | NATURAL RELEASE

1 Preheat the Instant Pot insert on SAUTÉ. Add 2 tablespoons of the vegetable oil and heat until it thins out.

2 Add mushrooms, celery, onion, bell pepper, and garlic and sauté for 5 minutes, just until vegetables begin to cook down. Remove and set aside.

3 Heat the remaining tablespoon of vegetable oil. Generously season steak with salt and pepper before browning on both sides.

4 Pour in beef stock and deglaze the insert before stirring in cooked vegetables, diced tomatoes, Worcestershire sauce, sugar, and celery salt.

5 Secure lid and seal pressure release vent.

6 Set Instant Pot to MEAT/STEW on HIGH pressure for 30 minutes.

7 Once cook time has elapsed, let the pressure release through NATURAL RELEASE.

8 Remove steak and set aside. Set Instant Pot to SAUTÉ. Whisk cornstarch into 2 tablespoons of water and stir into the cooking liquid. Bring up to a simmer and, stirring constantly, let cook 1 minute to thicken.

9 Adjust seasoning with additional salt and pepper to taste. Return steak to the sauce before serving topped with chopped parsley.

Just the Basics

For a full meal, serve this over white rice or homemade mashed potatoes.

Notes

Meat Loaf

The only thing this meat loaf is missing is . . . the loaf pan! To maximize the space inside the Instant Pot, I form this into a round loaf that sits atop the cooker's steam rack. The steamy environment inside the Instant Pot ensures the meat stays moist, even when using lean ground beef.

Ingredients

2 pounds lean ground beef

1 cup panko bread crumbs

1/3 cup minced yellow onion

1/4 cup ketchup

2 large eggs

3 tablespoons half-and-half

1 tablespoon Worcestershire sauce

2 teaspoons Dijon mustard

3/4 teaspoon garlic powder

3/4 teaspoon onion powder

1/2 teaspoon dried thyme

1 teaspoon salt

1/2 teaspoon pepper

TOPPING

1/2 cup ketchup

2 tablespoons dark brown sugar

MEAT/STEW | HIGH PRESSURE | 30 MINUTES | NATURAL RELEASE

1 Pour 1 cup of water into the Instant Pot insert and then place a steam rack over top.

2 In a large mixing bowl, combine all ingredients, except Topping ingredients. Knead together with your hands to mix and firmly pack everything together.

3 Form into a tall, round loaf about 7-inches wide. Be sure it is small enough around to fit atop your steam rack.

4 Lay out a square of aluminum foil and place the meat loaf in the center. Fold the edges up to make an aluminum bowl for the loaf. Do not wrap the top of the loaf. Transfer to the steam rack in the insert.

5 Secure lid and seal pressure release vent.

6 Set Instant Pot to MEAT/STEW on HIGH pressure for 30 minutes.

7 Once cook time has elapsed, let the pressure release through NATURAL RELEASE for 10 minutes before quick releasing any remaining pressure.

8 Transfer meat loaf to a sheet pan. Whisk together ketchup and brown sugar to make the Topping and brush over the top of the loaf.

9 Place oven rack in the second position from the top and set to BROIL. Place meat loaf under the broiler and cook 3 to 4 minutes, just until the Topping is bubbly hot and begins to brown.

Make it My Way

Lean ground beef is used because the steamy environment of the Instant Pot naturally keeps the meat loaf moist. Higher-fat ground beef will leave you with a lot of excess grease surrounding the finished loaf.

Just the Basics

Instant Pot's new Air Fryer Lid also can be used to brown the Topping. Lock the lid in place and set to BROIL for 3 minutes or until Topping is bubbly hot and beginning to brown.

Notes

Pulled Pork

Pulled pork is a staple of pressure cooking, as you can make it in only an hour, rather than the 4 hours it would take to make any other way. I like to make mine with cola in place of water as it ensures the results are even more tender and sweet. It's one of my husband Chris' favorite meals!

Ingredients

1 (3-pound) pork shoulder roast

Salt and pepper

2 tablespoons vegetable oil, divided

1 (12-ounce) can cola

2 cups barbecue sauce, divided

1/4 cup cider vinegar

3 tablespoons light brown sugar

2 teaspoons garlic powder

1 teaspoon onion powder

MEAT/STEW | HIGH PRESSURE | 60 MINUTES | NATURAL RELEASE

1 Cut pork roast into 6 equal-size pieces and generously season with salt and pepper on all sides.

2 Preheat the Instant Pot insert on SAUTÉ. Add 1 tablespoon of the vegetable oil and heat until it thins out.

3 Transfer 3 of the roast pieces to the Instant Pot and brown on at least 2 sides. Remove and set aside.

4 Repeat the last step with the remaining tablespoon of vegetable oil and the last 3 pieces of the roast. Remove and set aside.

5 Deglaze the insert with the cola and stir in 1/2 cup of the barbecue sauce and all of the cider vinegar, brown sugar, garlic powder, and onion powder. Return the roast to the pot and toss in the sauce.

6 Secure lid and seal pressure release vent.

7 Set Instant Pot to MEAT/STEW on HIGH pressure for 60 minutes.

8 Once cook time has elapsed, let the pressure release through NATURAL RELEASE.

9 Drain all but 1/2 cup of the cooking liquid before adding the remaining 1 1/2 cups of barbecue sauce. Using two forks, pull the pork into the sauce before serving.

Just the Basics

While it's hard to beat a classic pulled pork sandwich, this is also great over rice, atop nacho chips, or even over French fries!

Make it My Way

I like to let the pulled meat sit in the sauce for 15 minutes before serving.

Notes

MEATS

Apricot-Glazed Corned Beef

While most of us are pretty familiar with corned beef and cabbage, we rarely think of corned beef as a cut of meat that can be prepared in more unique ways. As corned beef is heavily brined (like a saltwater marinade), a sweet glaze over the top can perfectly offset that savory flavor. I like to use apricot preserves with just a pinch of red pepper flakes for a touch of heat.

Ingredients

1 (3- to 4-pound) corned beef brisket

1 tablespoon vegetable oil

Pepper

2 cups chicken stock

1 tablespoon apple cider vinegar

1/2 cup apricot preserves

1 tablespoon soy sauce (use tamari for gluten-free)

1/4 teaspoon crushed red pepper flakes

MEAT/STEW | HIGH PRESSURE | 75 MINUTES | NATURAL RELEASE

1 Discard any pickling spice packet that may have come with the corned beef and rinse the brisket under running water. Pat dry with paper towels.

2 Preheat the Instant Pot insert on SAUTÉ. Add vegetable oil and heat until oil is thin and hot.

3 Generously season the corned beef with pepper and add to the cooker, browning on both sides.

4 Remove brisket and deglaze the insert using chicken stock before stirring in apple cider vinegar. Turn off cooker.

5 Place corned beef on a steam rack. In a small bowl, whisk together apricot preserves, soy sauce, and crushed red pepper flakes. Spread over top of the corned beef.

6 Lower the steam rack with corned beef into the pot, over top of the cooking liquid. Secure lid and seal pressure release vent.

7 Set Instant Pot to MEAT/STEW on HIGH pressure for 75 minutes.

8 Once cook time has elapsed, let the pressure release through NATURAL RELEASE.

9 Remove corned beef from the pot and let rest 10 minutes before slicing to serve.

Just the Basics

Always slice any kind of beef "against the grain," which is the opposite direction of the fibers within the meat. You should be able to see long lines throughout the full cut of beef, and you want to cut through those lines, not alongside them.

Notes

MEATS

Beef Burgundy

Julia Child didn't create Beef Bourguignon, but she certainly made it one of the most popular French dishes in North America. What really sets it apart from other braised beef stews (besides a whole lot of red wine) is browning the beef in bacon grease.

Ingredients

1 tablespoon olive oil

6 strips bacon, chopped

2 pounds beef stew meat

Salt and pepper

1 tablespoon minced garlic

2 cups burgundy wine

1½ cups beef stock

2 tablespoons tomato paste

1 bay leaf

2 teaspoons sugar

¾ teaspoon onion powder

8 ounces baby bella mushrooms, halved

3 carrots, coarsely chopped

1 cup frozen pearl onions

2 tablespoons cornstarch

3 tablespoons water

MEAT/STEW | HIGH PRESSURE | 40 MINUTES | QUICK RELEASE

1 Preheat the Instant Pot insert on SAUTÉ. Add olive oil and bacon and sauté until crisp. Remove bacon and set aside.

2 Generously season the stew meat with salt and pepper. Transfer to the hot bacon grease in the insert and brown on at least 2 sides. For the best results, do this in 2 batches. Add garlic in the last minute of browning the meat and sauté along with it.

3 Deglaze the insert with the burgundy before stirring in the cooked bacon, beef stock, tomato paste, bay leaf, sugar, and onion powder.

4 Secure lid, and seal pressure release vent. Set Instant Pot to MEAT/STEW on HIGH pressure for 30 minutes.

5 Once cook time has elapsed, carefully perform a QUICK RELEASE of the pressure.

6 Stir in mushrooms and carrots before securing lid and sealing pressure release vent.

7 Set Instant Pot to MEAT/STEW on HIGH pressure for 10 minutes.

8 Once cook time has elapsed, carefully perform a QUICK RELEASE of the pressure.

9 Set Instant Pot to SAUTÉ and stir in pearl onions. Bring up to a simmer. Whisk cornstarch into 3 tablespoons of water and stir into the simmering stew. Let cook 1 minute or until thickened before seasoning with salt and pepper to taste.

MEATS

Just the Basics

Any dry red wine can be used in place of the burgundy.

Notes

Short Ribs with Plums

You don't need to go to an upscale restaurant to enjoy this high-quality dish with savory chuck short ribs and fresh sweet plums. The plums cook right into the gravy, giving it a flavor and sweetness that is unique, delicious, and hard to pin down. . . . But in the best of ways!

Ingredients

2 tablespoons vegetable oil

4–6 bone-in chuck short ribs

Salt and pepper

1/2 cup diced red onion

1 tablespoon minced garlic

2/3 cup beef stock

1 tablespoon balsamic vinegar

2 tablespoons sugar

3 sprigs fresh thyme

3 plums, halved and pitted

1 1/2 tablespoons cornstarch

2 tablespoons water

3 tablespoons butter

MEAT/STEW | HIGH PRESSURE | 45 MINUTES | NATURAL RELEASE

1 Preheat the Instant Pot insert on SAUTÉ. Add the vegetable oil and heat until it thins out.

2 Generously season the short ribs with salt and pepper and place in the Instant Pot, browning on at least 2 sides. You may need to do this in 2 batches.

3 Remove short ribs and sauté onion and garlic for 1 minute before deglazing the insert with beef stock.

4 Stir in balsamic vinegar, sugar, and thyme. Return short ribs to the pot and top with plums.

5 Secure lid and seal pressure release vent.

6 Set Instant Pot to MEAT/STEW on HIGH pressure for 45 minutes.

7 Once cook time has elapsed, let the pressure release through NATURAL RELEASE.

8 Remove short ribs and set aside. Set Instant Pot to SAUTÉ and bring up to a simmer. Whisk cornstarch into 2 tablespoons of water and then stir into the simmering cooking liquid, breaking up the plums as you stir. Let cook 1 minute, just until thickened. Turn off cooker.

9 With the heat off, stir in butter before seasoning the gravy with salt and pepper to taste. Return the short ribs to the gravy before serving.

MEATS

Just the Basics

If using boneless short ribs, simply lower the cook time to 40 minutes.

Notes

Instant Pot Lasagna

This lasagna is the perfect size to feed a family of four without having to buy two packages of most of the main ingredients, as you would to bake a lasagna in a 13 x 9-inch casserole dish.

Ingredients

Nonstick cooking spray

1 tablespoon olive oil

1 pound ground Italian
sausage or ground beef

1 tablespoon minced garlic

1/2 teaspoon salt

1/4 teaspoon pepper

1/4 teaspoon onion powder

1 1/2 cups shredded mozzarella
cheese, divided

1 cup ricotta cheese

1 large egg, beaten

1/4 cup grated Parmesan cheese

3/4 teaspoon Italian seasoning

1/4 teaspoon garlic powder

8 flat no-boil lasagna noodles

1 (24-ounce) jar pasta sauce

ACCESSORIES

7 x 3-inch springform pan

Just the Basics

I often make this in a 7-cup (1.7-liter) Anchor Hocking tempered-glass bowl. It makes for a very nice presentation, but you should not place glass under the broiler! Instead, you can bake the cooked lasagna for 10 minutes at 400°F to lightly brown the cheese.

PRESSURE COOK | HIGH PRESSURE | 35 MINUTES | NATURAL RELEASE

1 Spray a 7 x 3-inch springform pan with nonstick cooking spray. Fully wrap the outside and bottom of the pan with aluminum foil to prevent leaking.

2 Preheat the Instant Pot insert on SAUTÉ. Add olive oil and heat until it thins out. Place ground sausage or beef, garlic, salt, pepper, and onion powder in the insert and cook until fully browned. Drain excess grease and remove from insert, setting aside. Fully deglaze insert and wipe clean.

3 In a mixing bowl, fold together 1 cup of the mozzarella cheese and all of the ricotta cheese, egg, Parmesan cheese, Italian seasoning, and garlic powder.

4 Pour a thin layer (about 1/5 of the jar) of the pasta sauce into the bottom of the prepared pan and top with 2 lasagna noodles, breaking them to fit the round dish.

5 Top the noodles with 1/3 of the cheese mixture and spread gently. Top the cheese with 1/3 of the ground meat. Top the meat with 1/5 of the pasta sauce. Finally, top the sauce with 2 lasagna noodles.

6 Repeat the last step 2 more times to create three full layers with noodles on top. Pour the last 1/5 of the sauce over the noodles and top with the remaining 1/2 cup of mozzarella cheese.

7 Cover pan with aluminum foil. Pour 1 cup of water into the Instant Pot insert. Set the springform pan on a steam rack in insert. Secure lid and seal pressure release vent.

8 Set Instant Pot to PRESSURE COOK on HIGH for 35 minutes. Once cook time has elapsed, let the pressure release through NATURAL RELEASE.

9 Remove aluminum foil from the top of the pan and place lasagna under the broiler for 5 minutes, just until cheese is bubbly and beginning to brown. You also can do this with the BROIL setting on Instant Pot's new Air Fryer Lid. Let stand at least 5 minutes before slicing to serve.

MEATS

Notes

Pork Chops with Mushroom Gravy

These family-friendly pork chops use condensed mushroom soup to thicken the gravy but start with a ton of fresh ingredients to ensure a truly homemade taste.

Ingredients

2 tablespoons vegetable oil

8 ounces button
mushrooms, quartered

1/2 cup diced yellow onion

2 teaspoons minced garlic

1 tablespoon butter

4 bone-in pork chops
(about 3/4-inch thick)

Salt and pepper

3/4 cup beef stock

1 tablespoon chopped fresh sage

1 bay leaf

1 teaspoon Worcestershire sauce

1/2 teaspoon onion powder

1 (10.75-ounce) can condensed
cream of mushroom soup

Chopped fresh parsley,
for garnish

MEAT/STEW | HIGH PRESSURE | 6 MINUTES | NATURAL RELEASE

1 Preheat the Instant Pot insert on SAUTÉ. Add the vegetable oil and heat until it thins out.

2 Add mushrooms, onion, and garlic to the insert and sauté for 5 minutes, just until vegetables begin to cook down. Remove and set aside.

3 Add the butter to the insert, heating until sizzling hot. Generously season pork chops with salt and pepper before browning on both sides.

4 Deglaze the insert with the beef stock before stirring in cooked vegetables, sage, bay leaf, Worcestershire sauce, and onion powder.

5 Secure lid and seal pressure release vent. Set Instant Pot to MEAT/STEW on HIGH pressure for 6 minutes.

6 Once cook time has elapsed, let the pressure release through a NATURAL RELEASE for 10 minutes before quick releasing the remaining pressure.

7 Remove pork chops and set aside. Set Instant Pot to SAUTÉ, stir in condensed soup (do not add water to the soup) and bring up to a simmer.

8 Season sauce with salt and pepper to taste. Toss pork chops in sauce before serving topped with chopped parsley.

Just the Basics

For an even thicker gravy, whisk 1 tablespoon of cornstarch into 2 tablespoons of water and stir into the simmering gravy after adding the condensed soup. Let simmer 1 minute to thicken.

Notes

MEATS

Cuban Pork with Orange and Garlic

This tropical version of pulled pork is cooked right in a simple Cuban marinade called Mojo Criollo, an irresistible combination of orange juice, lime, oregano, cumin, and tons of fresh garlic. The secret to the rich flavor is to break a normal kitchen rule by NOT sautéing the garlic before cooking under pressure.

Ingredients

1 (3-pound) pork shoulder roast

Salt and pepper

2 tablespoons olive oil, divided

1 cup chicken stock

1 cup orange juice

Juice of 1 lime

2 tablespoons minced garlic

1½ tablespoons sugar

2 teaspoons orange zest

2 teaspoons dried oregano

1¼ teaspoons ground cumin

1 teaspoon onion powder

MEAT/STEW | HIGH PRESSURE | 60 MINUTES | NATURAL RELEASE

1 Cut pork roast into 6 equal-size pieces and heavily season with salt and pepper on all sides.

2 Preheat the Instant Pot insert on SAUTÉ. Add 1 tablespoon of the olive oil and heat until it thins out.

3 Transfer 3 of the roast pieces to the Instant Pot and brown on at least 2 sides. Remove and set aside.

4 Repeat the last step with the remaining tablespoon of olive oil and the last 3 pieces of the roast. Remove and set aside.

5 Deglaze the insert with the chicken stock and stir in orange juice, lime juice, garlic, sugar, orange zest, oregano, cumin, and onion powder. Add ¾ teaspoon each of salt and pepper.

6 Secure lid and seal pressure release vent.

7 Set Instant Pot to MEAT/STEW on HIGH pressure for 60 minutes.

8 Once cook time has elapsed, let the pressure release through NATURAL RELEASE.

9 Using two forks, pull the pork into the cooking liquid before serving.

MEATS

Just the Basics

For a full meal, serve alongside white or yellow rice and black beans. This is also great with sliced plantains, which you can find in the ethnic section of the freezer case of your local grocery store.

Notes

Smoked Pork Chops with Warm Apple Slaw

The warm slaw in this recipe is made with a sweet and tangy barbecue sauce that turns apples into something savory enough to serve alongside or smothered over smoked pork chops. You can cook the pork chops in the slaw, and they will come out fine. But I find that since they are already fully cooked, they stay juicier if I just let the hot slaw heat them through right before serving.

Ingredients

2 tablespoons vegetable oil, divided

4–8 boneless smoked pork chops (fully cooked)

1 yellow onion, thinly sliced

1 tablespoon smoked paprika

2 teaspoons minced garlic

½ cup chicken stock

1 (16-ounce) bag shredded coleslaw cabbage mix

2 apples, sliced

1 tablespoon cider vinegar

1 tablespoon brown sugar

¾ cup barbecue sauce

Salt and pepper to taste

PRESSURE COOK | HIGH PRESSURE | 1 MINUTE | QUICK RELEASE

1 Preheat the Instant Pot insert on SAUTÉ. Add 1 tablespoon of vegetable oil and heat until it thins out.

2 Add the pork chops to the cooker and brown on both sides. Remove and cover with aluminum foil.

3 Heat the remaining 1 tablespoon of vegetable oil in the insert and then add onion, paprika, and garlic. Sauté for 3 minutes, just until onion begins to turn translucent.

4 Pour in chicken stock and deglaze the insert before stirring in coleslaw mix, apples, cider vinegar, and brown sugar.

5 Secure lid and seal pressure release vent.

6 Set Instant Pot to PRESSURE COOK on HIGH pressure for 1 minute.

7 Once cook time has elapsed, carefully perform a QUICK RELEASE of the pressure.

8 Stir barbecue sauce into the cooked slaw and season with salt and pepper to taste.

9 Return the browned pork chops to the pot and fully cover them with the hot slaw. Loosely cover and let stand 2 minutes to heat the chops throughout before serving.

MEATS

Just the Basics

The type of fully cooked "pork chops" used in this recipe are closer in flavor and texture to ham and are often sold near the ham steaks.

Notes

Bolognese Sauce

This classic Bolognese Sauce builds flavors and richness as it slow cooks. The secret of the richness comes from two staples of a true bolognese—bacon and just a bit of milk.

Ingredients

1 tablespoon olive oil

1 1/2 pounds ground beef

3 slices bacon, diced

1 yellow onion, chopped

2 carrots, chopped

1 tablespoon minced garlic

1/2 cup beef stock

1 (28-ounce) can crushed tomatoes

1 tablespoon Italian seasoning

1 bay leaf

3/4 teaspoon salt

1/2 teaspoon pepper

1/2 cup milk

3 tablespoons tomato paste

SLOW COOK | LESS | 4 HOURS

1 Preheat the Instant Pot insert on SAUTÉ. Add olive oil and heat until it thins out.

2 Add ground beef and bacon and cook until beef has browned well. Drain excess grease.

3 Add onion, carrots, and garlic and sauté an additional 2 minutes before deglazing the pot with the beef stock. Turn off cooker.

4 Stir in crushed tomatoes, Italian seasoning, bay leaf, salt, and pepper. Cover with a glass lid.

5 Set Instant Pot to SLOW COOK on LESS for 4 hours.

6 Stir in milk and tomato paste in the last 15 minutes of the cook time.

Make it My Way

While bacon is a traditional and great addition to Bolognese Sauce, it can be omitted if you desire.

Just the Basics

When cooking with tomatoes, it's always a good idea to stir every hour or so and add water if the sauce is getting too thick.

Notes

MEATS

Hoisin-Glazed London Broil

London broil is an underused cut of steak that, when sous vide, will come out as tender and flavorful as any expensive steakhouse cut (think rib-eye). Many people overlook the cut because it is sometimes so big that it looks more like a roast than a steak, but you simply need to slice it thin after cooking.

Ingredients

1 London broil steak
(1½–2½ pounds)

¼ cup hoisin sauce, divided
(see Just the Basics)

2 tablespoons soy sauce, divided

1 teaspoon sesame oil

2 teaspoons minced garlic

Pepper

2 tablespoons vegetable oil

SOUS VIDE | 130°F | 2–4 HOURS

1 Place steam rack at the bottom of the Instant Pot insert and fill the insert with water to the MAX line. Place lid on Instant Pot.

2 Set Instant Pot to SOUS VIDE at 130°F for medium-rare, 135°F for medium, or 145°F for medium-well.

3 Set the cook time to a minimum of 2 hours, up to a maximum of 4 hours. Cooking results will be the same anytime within this window.

4 As the water preheats, place London broil, 2 tablespoons of the hoisin sauce, 1 tablespoon of the soy sauce, sesame oil, and garlic in a vacuum bag and seal.

5 Once water temperature is reached, submerge the bag in the water, secure lid on Instant Pot, and vent pressure valve to remain open. You may also cover with a glass lid.

6 Once cook time has elapsed, remove steak from bag and pat dry with paper towels. Season on both sides with pepper.

7 Drain Instant Pot insert and set to SAUTÉ. Allow at least 2 minutes to preheat before adding vegetable oil. Allow vegetable oil 1 minute to heat up. Sear the cooked steak on both sides, just until it begins to brown.

8 For the best flavor, carefully remove insert from Instant Pot (it is very hot) to immediately reduce the heat. Add remaining 2 tablespoons hoisin sauce and 1 tablespoon soy sauce and flip the steak in the sauces as they bubble up and caramelize onto the steak.

9 Let rest 5 minutes before thinly slicing against the grain.

Just the Basics

Like a Chinese barbecue sauce, hoisin is sold in small jars in the Asian foods aisle of grocery stores. It is the sweet and savory sauce that Chinese restaurants give you alongside Moo Shu dishes.

MEATS

Notes

Rosemary Pork Tenderloin

Pork tenderloin is the most tender (and lean) cut of pork with only one downside.... It cooks rapidly and can go from perfectly cooked to dry in a matter of minutes. Thankfully, when you are cooking sous vide the results are always perfectly cooked and ready on your schedule.

Ingredients

1–2 pork tenderloins
(about 1½ pounds)

Salt and pepper

Garlic powder

Zest of 1 lemon

2 large sprigs fresh rosemary

2 tablespoons olive oil

SOUS VIDE | 140°F | 2–4 HOURS

1 Place steam rack at the bottom of the Instant Pot insert and fill the insert with water to the MAX line. Place lid on Instant Pot.

2 Set Instant Pot to SOUS VIDE at 140°F for medium with pink in the center, 145°F for less pink (this is my favorite temperature), or 150°F for medium-well and very little pink.

3 Set the cook time to a minimum of 1 hour, up to a maximum of 4 hours. Cooking results will be the same anytime within this window.

4 As the water preheats, lightly season pork tenderloins with salt, pepper, and garlic powder and then rub with lemon zest. Place the seasoned tenderloins and fresh rosemary in a vacuum-seal bag and seal.

5 Once water temperature is reached, submerge the bag in the water, secure lid on Instant Pot, and vent pressure valve to remain open. You may also cover with a glass lid.

6 Once cook time has elapsed, remove tenderloins from bag and pat dry with paper towels. Season again with salt, pepper, and garlic powder.

7 Drain Instant Pot insert and set to SAUTÉ. Allow at least 2 minutes to preheat before adding olive oil. Allow olive oil at least 1 minute to heat up.

8 Sear the cooked tenderloins on at least 2 sides, just until they begin to brown. Remove immediately. Let rest 5 minutes before slicing to serve.

Just the Basics

Be sure to buy fresh pork tenderloin that is not marinated or seasoned. Fresh tenderloins are most often sold in a 2-pack, which will work great in this recipe.

MEATS

Notes

Balsamic-Glazed Top Sirloin

Sous vide was made for cooking steaks, and this simple recipe will allow you to create a restaurant-quality top sirloin filet right inside the Instant Pot. The temperatures and times below will actually work for any cut of steak, but I find that top sirloin filets are a great balance between tenderness, flavor, and cost. For a special occasion, try this method with filet mignon!

Ingredients

2 top sirloin filets

2 tablespoons balsamic glaze, divided

2 small sprigs thyme

Salt and pepper

1 tablespoon olive oil

SOUS VIDE | 130°F | 2-4 HOURS

1 Place steam rack at the bottom of the Instant Pot insert and fill the insert with water to the MAX line. Place lid on Instant Pot.

2 Set Instant Pot to SOUS VIDE at 130°F for medium-rare, 135°F for medium, or 145°F for medium-well.

3 Set the cook time to a minimum of 2 hours, up to a maximum of 4 hours. Cooking results will be the same anytime within this window.

4 As the water preheats, place sirloin filets, 1 tablespoon of the balsamic glaze, and thyme in a vacuum-seal bag and seal.

5 Once water temperature is reached, submerge the bag in the water, secure lid on Instant Pot, and vent pressure valve to remain open. You may also cover with a glass lid.

6 Once cook time has elapsed, remove steaks from bag and pat dry with paper towels. Season on both sides with salt and pepper.

7 Drain Instant Pot insert and set to SAUTÉ. Allow at least 2 minutes to preheat before adding olive oil. Allow olive oil at least 1 minute to heat up.

8 Sear the cooked steaks on both sides, just until they begin to brown. Remove immediately.

9 Toss the seared steaks in the remaining 1 tablespoon of balsamic glaze before serving.

Just the Basics

This recipe can be doubled easily to serve 4 people, though you may need to perform step of searing the cooked steaks on the stovetop or in 2 batches in the Instant Pot.

Notes

Poultry

pressure cook

sauté

sous vide

Chicken Pot Pie

As soon as you get that pesky piecrust out of the way, preparing a chicken pot pie can be pretty simple. For my recipe, I solve that pesky piecrust problem by replacing it with biscuits, which I bake as the filling is cooking under pressure.

Ingredients

2 tablespoons vegetable oil

1 tablespoon butter

1½ pounds boneless, skinless chicken breasts, chopped

1 small yellow onion, diced

2 cups chicken stock

2 medium Russet potatoes, chopped

1 bay leaf

¾ teaspoon dried thyme

½ teaspoon salt

¼ teaspoon pepper

¼ teaspoon poultry seasoning

¼ teaspoon garlic powder

2 cups frozen mixed vegetables

½ cup half-and-half

3 tablespoons cornstarch

¼ cup grated Parmesan cheese

4–8 cooked biscuits

Just the Basics

You can top this with any type of cooked biscuits, prepared according to the package directions. I typically prefer frozen biscuits over canned biscuits, and those are what are pictured at left.

MEAT/STEW | HIGH PRESSURE | 2 MINUTES | NATURAL RELEASE

1. Preheat the Instant Pot insert on SAUTÉ. Add vegetable oil and butter and heat until sizzling.

2. Add the chopped chicken breasts to the insert and sauté for 4 minutes, until it begins to lightly brown. Fold in diced onion and sauté 2 additional minutes.

3. Pour in chicken stock and deglaze the insert before stirring in potatoes, bay leaf, thyme, salt, pepper, poultry seasoning, and garlic powder.

4. Secure lid and seal pressure release vent.

5. Set Instant Pot to MEAT/STEW on HIGH pressure for 2 minutes.

6. Once cook time has elapsed, let the pressure release through NATURAL RELEASE for 5 minutes before quick releasing any remaining pressure.

7. Set Instant Pot to SAUTÉ and stir in frozen mixed vegetables. Bring up to a simmer.

8. Whisk together half-and-half and cornstarch before stirring into the cooking liquid. Let simmer, stirring constantly, 1 minute.

9. Turn off cooker and stir in Parmesan cheese before serving bowls topped with 1–2 cooked biscuits each.

Notes _____

Pulled Chicken Tacos

This recipe makes tender pulled chicken in picante sauce that you can use to stuff any taco, whether it is soft or hard. The Instant Pot can make the chicken tender enough to pull in only 15 minutes, which makes it pretty much on par with making standard ground beef taco filling on the stovetop.

Ingredients

1½ pounds boneless, skinless chicken breasts

1 tablespoon taco seasoning

1 cup chicken stock

1 tablespoon olive oil

1 cup picante sauce

Soft or hard taco shells

Shredded cheese, lettuce, or your favorite taco fixings

MEAT/STEW | HIGH PRESSURE | 15 MINUTES | NATURAL RELEASE

1 Rub the entire surface of the chicken breasts with taco seasoning before placing in the insert of the Instant Pot.

2 Pour chicken stock and olive oil into the insert.

3 Secure lid and seal pressure release vent.

4 Set Instant Pot to MEAT/STEW on HIGH pressure for 15 minutes.

5 Once cook time has elapsed, let the pressure release through NATURAL RELEASE.

6 Remove chicken breasts from cooking liquid and transfer to a mixing bowl. Pour picante sauce over top.

7 Using two forks, pull and shred the chicken into the picante sauce.

8 Serve the pulled chicken in soft or hard tortilla shells topped with shredded cheese, lettuce, additional picante sauce, or your favorite taco fixings.

Make it My Way

I also love to use this pulled chicken as a filling in homemade quesadillas with plenty of melted cheese.

POULTRY

Just the Basics

Pulled chicken needs a lot of moisture to soak up and will absorb most of the picante sauce. If you'd like saucier chicken, add a few tablespoons of the cooking liquid as you pull the meat.

Notes

Turkey Pot Roast

Sliced turkey breast is served with tender vegetables and smothered in gravy in this recipe, which you won't want to save for the holidays to prepare.

Ingredients

2 tablespoons vegetable oil

1 (4-pound) boneless, skinless turkey breast

1 tablespoon paprika

2 teaspoons dry rubbed sage

1 1/2 teaspoons dried thyme

3/4 teaspoon poultry seasoning

3/4 teaspoon onion powder

3/4 teaspoon salt

1/2 teaspoon pepper

1 cup chicken stock

1 bay leaf

2 sweet potatoes, cut into 3-inch chunks

3 medium carrots, peeled and chopped into 2-inch lengths

3 stalks celery, cut into 2-inch lengths

2 tablespoons all-purpose flour

1/4 cup half-and-half

MEAT/STEW | HIGH PRESSURE | 30 MINUTES | NATURAL RELEASE

1 Preheat the Instant Pot insert on SAUTÉ. Add vegetable oil and heat until it thins out.

2 Pat the turkey breast with paper towels and then season with paprika, sage, thyme, poultry seasoning, onion powder, salt, and pepper. Transfer to the insert and brown well on at least 1 side.

3 Remove turkey, deglaze the insert with the chicken stock, and add bay leaf before returning the turkey to the pot. Secure lid and seal pressure release vent.

4 Set Instant Pot to MEAT/STEW on HIGH pressure for 25 minutes.

5 Once cook time has elapsed, let the pressure release through NATURAL RELEASE.

6 Transfer turkey to a cutting board and cover with aluminum foil. Add the sweet potatoes, carrots, and celery to the cooking liquid in the insert. Set Instant Pot to PRESSURE COOK on HIGH pressure for 5 minutes.

7 Once cook time has elapsed, carefully perform a QUICK RELEASE of the pressure.

8 Transfer vegetables to a serving platter. Set the Instant Pot to SAUTÉ and bring up to a simmer. Whisk flour into half-and-half before whisking into the cooking liquid. Let simmer, whisking constantly, until thickened. Season gravy with salt and pepper to taste. Slice turkey and serve alongside vegetables. Cover turkey with the gravy.

Just the Basics

For a 3-pound turkey breast, reduce the initial cook time from 25 minutes to 20 minutes.

Notes —————————————————————————————————

POULTRY

Chicken Marsala

Boneless, skinless chicken breasts are served in a beefy mushroom cream sauce with a bit of sweetness coming from marsala wine. The secret to ensuring a bold flavor is to add wine before and after cooking under pressure, as the first measure ensures a deep flavor while the second adds brightness. The alcohol eventually cooks out (leaving only the flavor behind) as you bring the sauce to a simmer before serving.

Ingredients

4 boneless, skinless chicken breasts

¼ cup all-purpose flour

½ teaspoon salt

¼ teaspoon pepper

2 tablespoons olive oil

½ cup marsala cooking wine, divided

8 ounces baby bella mushrooms, quartered

½ cup diced red onion

2 teaspoons minced garlic

¼ teaspoon dried thyme

½ cup beef stock

¼ cup heavy cream

1 tablespoon cornstarch

Chopped fresh parsley, for garnish

MEAT/STEW | HIGH PRESSURE | 5 MINUTES | NATURAL RELEASE

1 Place chicken, flour, salt, and pepper in a food storage container or bag, and shake until chicken is evenly coated in flour.

2 Preheat the Instant Pot insert on SAUTÉ. Add the olive oil and heat until it thins out.

3 Place floured chicken in the Instant Pot and brown on both sides. You may need to do this in 2 batches, using additional olive oil. Remove chicken and set aside.

4 Deglaze the insert with ¼ cup of the marsala wine. As the wine is bubbling up, add mushrooms, onion, garlic, and thyme and sauté 2 minutes.

5 Pour in beef stock and deglaze the insert again before returning the chicken breasts to the pot.

6 Secure lid and seal pressure release vent. Set Instant Pot to MEAT/STEW on HIGH pressure for 5 minutes.

7 Once cook time has elapsed, let the pressure release through a NATURAL RELEASE for 5 minutes before quick releasing the remaining pressure.

8 Remove chicken and set aside. Set Instant Pot to SAUTÉ, stir in heavy cream, and bring up to a simmer.

9 Whisk cornstarch into the remaining ¼ cup of marsala wine and then stir into the simmering sauce. Let cook 1 minute, just until thickened. Season sauce with salt and pepper to taste. Toss chicken in sauce before serving topped with chopped parsley.

Just the Basics

For an even more flavorful sauce, a teaspoon of beef bouillon base (sold in small jars near the stocks and broths) can be stirred in along with the heavy cream.

POULTRY

Notes

Chicken Alfredo "Skillet" Meal

This family-friendly meal with a homemade Alfredo sauce can be made in only minutes under pressure and with very minimal prep work. For even less prep work, see the "Make it My Way" section below.

Ingredients

1 tablespoon butter

1 tablespoon vegetable oil

2 large boneless, skinless chicken breasts, chopped

1 tablespoon minced garlic

1/8 teaspoon ground nutmeg

4 cups chicken stock

1 pound penne pasta

1 1/2 cups frozen peas and carrots

1 cup grated Parmesan cheese

4 ounces cream cheese, softened

3/4 cup heavy cream

Salt and pepper to taste

Chopped fresh parsley, for garnish

PRESSURE COOK | HIGH PRESSURE | 5 MINUTES | QUICK RELEASE

1. Heat butter and vegetable oil in the Instant Pot set to SAUTÉ.

2. Add chicken and cook until lightly browned. Stir in garlic and nutmeg and cook 1 additional minute.

3. Stir in chicken stock and deglaze pan. Add penne pasta and ensure all pasta is just below the level of the liquid, adding slightly more if necessary.

4. Secure lid and seal pressure release vent.

5. Set Instant Pot to PRESSURE COOK on HIGH for 5 minutes.

6. As the pasta cooks, microwave frozen peas and carrots for 3 minutes, just until thawed and warmed through.

7. Once cook time has elapsed, carefully perform a QUICK RELEASE of the pressure.

8. Stir in peas and carrots, Parmesan cheese, cream cheese, and heavy cream before seasoning with salt and pepper to taste. Sauce will thicken slightly if you let it rest 5 minutes. Serve topped with chopped fresh parsley, if desired.

Make it My Way

This can be made with even less prep by skipping the first two steps and simply cooking the pasta with broth, garlic, and nutmeg. Then stir in precooked chicken (such as Perdue Short Cuts brand) as you stir in the vegetables.

Just the Basics

If the cheese and other ingredients cool things down too much, simply set the Instant Pot to SAUTÉ on LOW and stir constantly, just until hot. Immediately turn off cooker.

POULTRY

Notes _____

Chicken Cacciatore

I like to make this classic Italian dish of chicken stewed in tomatoes using bone-in chicken thighs, as they always come out super tender when cooking under pressure. For a full meal, serve over a hearty pasta (I like penne) or even white rice.

Ingredients

2 tablespoons olive oil

8 ounces baby bella mushrooms, quartered

1 small red onion, chopped

1 green bell pepper, chopped

2 carrots, chopped

1 tablespoon minced garlic

1 1/2 teaspoons Italian seasoning

1/2 cup chicken stock

1 (15-ounce) can diced tomatoes, with liquid

1/4 cup chopped fresh basil

1 tablespoon sugar

1/2 teaspoon salt

1/4 teaspoon pepper

2 pounds skinless, bone-in chicken thighs

3 tablespoons tomato paste

MEAT/STEW | HIGH PRESSURE | 15 MINUTES | NATURAL RELEASE

1 Preheat the Instant Pot insert on SAUTÉ. Add olive oil and heat until it thins out.

2 Add mushrooms, onion, bell pepper, carrots, garlic, and Italian seasoning and sauté for 5 minutes, just until vegetables begin to cook down.

3 Pour in chicken stock and deglaze the insert before stirring in diced tomatoes, basil, sugar, salt, and pepper.

4 Press the chicken thighs down into the sauce and then spoon tomato paste over top without stirring in.

5 Secure lid and seal pressure release vent.

6 Set Instant Pot to MEAT/STEW on HIGH pressure for 15 minutes.

7 Once cook time has elapsed, let the pressure release through NATURAL RELEASE.

8 Stir the tomato paste into the sauce and adjust seasoning with additional salt and pepper to taste before serving.

POULTRY

Just the Basics

If you would like to make this with the skin on, you should brown the chicken thighs in olive oil before cooking. This will need to be done separately from the vegetables to prevent overcrowding.

Notes

Chicken Burrito Bowls

This recipe starts with frozen chicken, dried beans, and uncooked brown rice—three ingredients notorious for taking a very long time to cook—and cooks them all at once under pressure in only 25 minutes. You then top them with classic burrito fixings for a restaurant-quality bowl that is sure to fill you up.

Ingredients

1½ pounds frozen boneless, skinless chicken breasts

1½ cups chicken stock

1 (14.5-ounce) can diced tomatoes, with liquid

½ cup uncooked brown rice

½ cup uncooked black beans

2 tablespoons minced garlic

1 tablespoon olive oil

1 tablespoon chili powder

2 teaspoons onion powder

½ teaspoon salt

Shredded Mexican cheese blend

1 avocado, sliced

1 cup fresh salsa

½ cup sour cream

PRESSURE COOK | HIGH PRESSURE | 25 MINUTES | QUICK RELEASE

1   In the Instant Pot insert, toss to combine frozen chicken, chicken stock, diced tomatoes, brown rice, black beans, garlic, olive oil, chili powder, onion powder, and salt.

2   Secure lid and seal pressure release vent.

3   Set Instant Pot to PRESSURE COOK on HIGH pressure for 25 minutes.

4   Once cook time has elapsed, carefully perform a QUICK RELEASE of the pressure.

5   Using two forks, pull and shred the chicken into the rice and beans in the cooker.

6   Spoon into 4 large serving bowls and top with an equal amount of the shredded cheese, sliced avocado, fresh salsa, and sour cream.

Make it My Way

I really like to make this as a salad as well. I start by placing chopped romaine lettuce in each serving bowl before topping with the hot ingredients and then the cheese, avocado, salsa, and sour cream.

Just the Basics

I would only recommend making this with frozen chicken, not fresh, as you need a long enough cook time to ensure that the rice and beans cook up tender.

Notes ——————————————————————————

POULTRY

Chicken Sausage and Rice Divan   NO

Chicken Divan is a classic casserole with cheese and broccoli that often includes rice (as it does here). My twist on the classic is to start with smoked chicken sausage, rather than raw chicken. It makes for easier prep and even more flavor than traditional Divan.

Ingredients

1 tablespoon vegetable oil

1 tablespoon butter

4 links smoked chicken sausage, sliced

3/4 cup diced yellow onion

1 1/2 cups chicken stock

1 1/2 cups long grain white rice, rinsed

1/4 teaspoon garlic powder

Pinch nutmeg

1 cup milk

8 ounces processed cheese (Velveeta), chopped

12 ounces frozen broccoli florets, thawed

Salt and pepper to taste

RICE | HIGH PRESSURE | LESS | NATURAL RELEASE

1 Preheat the Instant Pot insert on SAUTÉ. Add vegetable oil and butter and heat until sizzling.

2 Add chicken sausage and onion and sauté until sausage begins to brown and onion is translucent. Remove and set aside until after the rice is cooked.

3 Pour in chicken stock and deglaze the insert before stirring in rice, garlic powder, and nutmeg.

4 Secure lid and seal pressure release vent.

5 Set Instant Pot to RICE on HIGH pressure on the LESS preset.

6 Once cook time has elapsed, let the pressure release through NATURAL RELEASE for 10 minutes before quick releasing any remaining pressure.

7 Stir milk and processed cheese into the rice until melted and combined.

8 Fold in broccoli florets and cooked sausage and onion before seasoning with salt and pepper to taste.

Just the Basics

The rice will be very hot after pressure cooking and should fully heat the remaining ingredients. If it cools down too much, simply set to SAUTÉ on the LESS preset and cook, stirring constantly, just until hot. Turn off cooker and serve immediately.

Notes

Swedish Turkey Meatballs

Frozen turkey meatballs are the perfect choice for making Swedish Meatballs in the Instant Pot, as they hold their shape much better than homemade meatballs when stacked on top of each other, usually aren't heavily seasoned with Italian herbs as most packaged beef meatballs are, and don't release a ton of grease into the cooking liquid, which you need to create the irresistible gravy.

Ingredients

24 ounces frozen turkey meatballs

1 cup beef stock

1 tablespoon butter, melted

1 teaspoon Worcestershire sauce

1/4 teaspoon ground allspice

Pinch nutmeg

3 tablespoons all-purpose flour

3/4 cup heavy cream

2 teaspoons Dijon mustard

1/2 teaspoon onion powder

1/4 teaspoon salt

1/4 teaspoon pepper

1/4 cup chopped fresh parsley, for garnish

PRESSURE COOK | HIGH PRESSURE | 5 MINUTES | QUICK RELEASE

1 In the Instant Pot insert, stir to combine turkey meatballs, beef stock, butter, Worcestershire sauce, allspice, and nutmeg.

2 Secure lid and seal pressure release vent.

3 Set Instant Pot to PRESSURE COOK on HIGH pressure for 5 minutes.

4 Once cook time has elapsed, carefully perform a QUICK RELEASE of the pressure.

5 Remove meatballs and set aside.

6 Set Instant Pot to SAUTÉ and bring cooking liquid up to a simmer.

7 Whisk flour into heavy cream and then whisk into the simmering cooking liquid. Stir in Dijon mustard, onion powder, salt, and pepper.

8 Stirring constantly, let cook 3 minutes, until thickened.

9 Fold in cooked meatballs and serve topped with chopped fresh parsley.

Just the Basics

For even more flavor in the sauce, add a teaspoon of concentrated beef base (sold in small jars near the stocks and broths). You may want to reduce the salt to 1/4 teaspoon though, as the base is high in sodium.

Make it My Way

Swedish meatballs are typically served with lingonberry jam, but you can only find that at specialty stores or online. I find that the closest thing is canned whole-berry cranberry sauce (not the jelly type of sauce). Not only are cranberries in the same family as lingonberries, but also they go great with turkey!

POULTRY

Notes _____

121

Cashew Chicken Stir Fry

This simple stir fry cooks so quickly that there's no need to cook it under pressure. Simply set the Instant Pot to Sauté and enjoy takeout-quality Chinese food in less than 15 minutes. The best part is that there's only one pot to clean!

Ingredients

3 tablespoons vegetable oil

1 pound boneless, skinless chicken breasts, chopped

3 tablespoons cornstarch

12 ounces broccoli florets

1 small red bell pepper, chopped

2 teaspoons minced garlic

$1/3$ cup raw cashews

$1/4$ cup low-sodium soy sauce

2 tablespoons honey

$1/4$ teaspoon crushed red pepper flakes, optional

1 tablespoon sesame oil

$1/4$ cup chopped scallions

SAUTÉ | 12 MINUTES

1 Preheat the Instant Pot insert on SAUTÉ. Add vegetable oil and heat until it thins out.

2 Toss chopped chicken breast in cornstarch until all pieces are lightly coated. Discard any excess cornstarch.

3 Add the coated chicken to the insert and sauté until lightly browned, about 4 minutes.

4 Stir in broccoli, bell pepper, and garlic and sauté an additional 3 minutes.

5 Stir in cashews, soy sauce, honey, and pepper flakes. Cover with a glass lid and let steam for 3 minutes.

6 Remove lid and stir constantly until the soy sauce and honey have thickened and broccoli is crisp-tender.

7 Turn off heat and stir in sesame oil before serving topped with chopped scallions.

Make it My Way

I like the crushed red pepper flakes, as it adds a very slight heat to offset the honey; but it can be omitted if you'd prefer to keep things mild.

POULTRY

Just the Basics

The sesame oil is added after cooking, as much of the flavor of sesame oil cooks out at a high heat.

Notes

123

Greek Chicken Pitas

Pitas are filled with a sautéed version of Chicken Souvlaki (chicken with lemon, garlic, and oregano) in this quick and easy Greek dinner. Served over a pita, it's a prerequisite that you pile on plenty of tzatziki sauce, a cool and creamy sauce made from Greek yogurt, cucumbers, and dill.

Ingredients

- 1 pound boneless, skinless chicken breasts
- 3 tablespoons olive oil, divided
- Juice of ½ lemon
- 2 teaspoons minced garlic
- 1 teaspoon dried oregano
- 1 teaspoon sugar
- ½ teaspoon salt
- ¼ teaspoon pepper
- 1 yellow onion, thinly sliced
- 4 rounds pita bread or pita pockets
- Tzatziki sauce (see below)
- Chopped lettuce
- Chopped tomatoes
- Crumbled feta cheese, optional

SAUTÉ | 10 MINUTES

1. Chop chicken into 1-inch chunks before tossing in 1 tablespoon of the olive oil and all of the lemon juice, garlic, oregano, sugar, salt, and pepper. Cover and refrigerate for 15 minutes to marinate.

2. Preheat the Instant Pot insert on SAUTÉ. Add remaining olive oil and heat until it thins out.

3. Add the marinated chicken to the insert and sauté 5 minutes, letting it lightly brown.

4. Add yellow onion and sauté an additional 4 minutes, until onion is tender and chicken is cooked throughout.

5. Serve chicken and onion on pita bread topped with tzatziki sauce, lettuce, tomatoes, and feta cheese, if desired.

Tzatziki Sauce

They sell premade tzatziki sauce near the prepared hummus in most grocery stores. You can make your own tzatziki sauce by tossing ½ cup of finely diced cucumber in ¼ teaspoon salt and placing on paper towels to drain as the salt pulls out excess moisture. Stir this into 1 cup of plain Greek yogurt and add 3 tablespoons of chopped fresh dill. Season with salt and pepper to taste.

Just the Basics

If your chicken is sticking to the Instant Pot insert, leave it be, and it will brown and then release itself.

Notes

POULTRY

Olive Oil-Poached Chicken Breasts

Poaching chicken breasts in oil on the stove wastes a lot of oil, can get messy, and can even get dangerous if you don't watch the temperature of the oil. Poaching by using the Instant Pot's sous vide function fixes all of those issues and creates the juiciest chicken breasts I've ever had. It's an especially great way to cook batches of chicken to chop and use in other recipes or to top salads.

Ingredients

4 boneless, skinless
   chicken breasts

1/4 cup extra-virgin olive oil

4 cloves garlic

2 sprigs fresh thyme

1 teaspoon salt

1/2 teaspoon whole
   black peppercorns

SOUS VIDE | 150°F | 1 1/2–4 HOURS

1 Place steam rack at the bottom of the Instant Pot insert and fill the insert with water to the MAX line. Place lid on Instant Pot.

2 Set Instant Pot to SOUS VIDE at 150°F.

3 Set the cook time to a minimum of 90 minutes, up to a maximum of 4 hours. Cooking results will be the same anytime within this window.

4 As the water preheats, place chicken breasts and all ingredients in a vacuum-seal bag and toss to disperse the salt. Seal bag.

5 Once water temperature is reached, submerge the bag in the water, secure lid on Instant Pot, and vent pressure valve to remain open. You may also cover with a glass lid.

6 Once cook time has elapsed, remove chicken from oil and serve as is or continue on to lightly brown.

7 Drain Instant Pot insert and set to SAUTÉ. Allow at least 2 minutes to preheat.

8 Toss chicken in the cooking oil and place in the cooker, searing until lightly browned on at least one side. Lightly season with additional salt and ground pepper and immediately remove from the pot to serve.

Just the Basics

Truly poached chicken is very mild in flavor and isn't browned on the outside, but I prefer just a little bit of color from a light sear and the extra flavor that that brings.

POULTRY

Notes

Turkey Tenderloins with Maple Pan Sauce

Most grocery stores now carry fresh turkey tenderloins in the poultry section. It's a lean and modest cut of meat that allows you to enjoy carved turkey outside of the holidays without roasting an entire bird. It can be a tricky cut of meat to cook correctly, making it a perfect candidate for making sous vide.

Ingredients

1–2 pounds turkey tenderloins

4 leaves fresh sage

1 tablespoon butter, melted

2 tablespoons pure maple syrup

1 tablespoon soy sauce
(tamari for gluten-free)

⅛ teaspoon ground cinnamon

2 tablespoons vegetable oil

Salt and pepper

2 tablespoons butter

Just the Basics

This is best when made using fresh turkey tenderloins, not ones that are pre-marinated. Small boneless turkey breasts will also work.

SOUS VIDE | 145°F | 2–4 HOURS

1 Place steam rack at the bottom of the Instant Pot insert and fill the insert with water to the MAX line. Place lid on Instant Pot.

2 Set Instant Pot to SOUS VIDE at 145°F for a minimum of 2 hours, up to a maximum of 4 hours. Cooking results will be the same anytime within this window.

3 As the water preheats, place turkey tenderloins in a vacuum-seal bag and top with sage leaves. Whisk together melted butter, maple syrup, soy sauce, and cinnamon and pour into the bag before sealing.

4 Once water temperature is reached, submerge the bag in the water, secure lid on Instant Pot, and vent pressure valve to remain open. You may also cover with a glass lid.

5 Once cook time has elapsed, remove turkey from bag and pat dry with paper towels. Reserve cooking liquid in bag.

6 Drain Instant Pot insert and set to SAUTÉ. Allow at least 2 minutes to preheat before adding vegetable oil. Allow vegetable oil 1 minute to heat up.

7 Lightly season turkey tenderloins with salt and pepper and sear each on at least 2 sides, just until beginning to brown. Remove and let rest.

8 Deglaze the Instant Pot insert with the cooking liquid from the vacuum bag, bringing it up to a simmer and letting cook 1 minute. Turn off heat and stir in 2 tablespoons of butter to make a quick pan sauce.

9 Slice turkey tenderloins and serve drizzled with the pan sauce.

POULTRY

Notes

Seafood

pressure cook

slow cook

sauté

sous vide

SEAFOOD

Low Country Boil

This was the second recipe I ever made in the Instant Pot. Back then, it was the first time I had attempted any seafood boil using any cooking method. I found it so simple and flavorful that I've been making it ever since! I even bring my Instant Pot with me on vacation in the Outer Banks of North Carolina, just to prepare this recipe. I like to keep it simple by making this using only shrimp, as my husband and I typically do not eat the clams or mussels that are in other seafood boil recipes.

Ingredients

14 ounces smoked sausage, cut into 1-inch lengths

3 ears corn, cut into thirds

1½ pounds small red potatoes, halved

1½ pounds frozen peeled large raw shrimp

2 cups hot water

¼ cup Buffalo wing sauce

1½ tablespoons Old Bay seasoning

½ teaspoon garlic powder

3 tablespoons butter, sliced

Chopped parsley, for garnish

Lemon wedges, for garnish

STEAM | HIGH PRESSURE | 5 MINUTES | QUICK RELEASE

1 Place sausage, corn, potatoes, and shrimp in the Instant Pot insert.

2 In a mixing bowl, whisk together water, Buffalo sauce, Old Bay seasoning, and garlic powder. Pour over the ingredients in the Instant Pot and toss gently.

3 Secure lid and seal pressure release vent.

4 Set Instant Pot to STEAM on HIGH pressure for 5 minutes.

5 Once cook time has elapsed, carefully perform a QUICK RELEASE of the pressure.

6 Serve topped with butter, parsley, and lemon wedges.

Make it My Way

I prefer to use frozen peeled shrimp, but you also can prepare this with shell-on shrimp, and the shells will bring slightly more flavor to the broth.

SEAFOOD

Just the Basics

For a more robust flavor but less broth, reduce the water mixed into the Buffalo sauce to 1 cup.

Notes

Tuna Casserole

My Instant Pot take on this casserole classic is still as simple to make as you'd expect but includes a sauce that is entirely made from scratch. There's one secret ingredient I don't make from scratch: I use crushed croutons sprinkled over top to replicate the crunchy bread-crumb topping of an oven-baked casserole.

Ingredients

1 tablespoon butter

1 tablespoon vegetable oil

8 ounces button
 mushrooms, sliced

3/4 cup diced yellow onion

2 teaspoons minced garlic

4 cups chicken stock

1 pound bow tie pasta

1/2 teaspoon onion powder

1/2 teaspoon dried thyme

1 1/2 cups frozen peas

2/3 cup heavy cream

3/4 cup grated Parmesan cheese

3 (5-ounce) cans tuna, drained

Salt and pepper to taste

1 cup crushed croutons

PRESSURE COOK | HIGH PRESSURE | 5 MINUTES | QUICK RELEASE

1 Heat butter and vegetable oil in the Instant Pot set to SAUTÉ.

2 Add mushrooms, onion, and garlic and sauté 4 minutes, just until mushrooms begin to soften.

3 Pour in chicken stock and deglaze the insert before stirring in bow tie pasta, onion powder, and thyme.

4 Secure lid and seal pressure release vent.

5 Set Instant Pot to PRESSURE COOK on HIGH for 5 minutes.

6 Once cook time has elapsed, carefully perform a QUICK RELEASE of the pressure.

7 Set Instant Pot to SAUTÉ and stir in peas and heavy cream. Let cook, stirring constantly, just until peas are warmed through.

8 Turn off cooker and stir in Parmesan cheese before folding in canned tuna.

9 Season with salt and pepper to taste before serving topped with crushed croutons.

Just the Basics

This is also great if made with canned or refrigerated jumbo lump crab meat (sold in small tubs near the fresh seafood case) in place of the tuna.

Notes

SEAFOOD

Pesto Salmon

When cooking fish under pressure, flavor is fundamental. As the fish is being steamed and will not be browned, you need something robust to build up the flavor. In this case, I use a simple store-bought pesto sauce to bring that flavor, which actually infuses into the salmon like a marinade in only 3 minutes under pressure!

Ingredients

4 wedges or slices lemon

Nonstick cooking spray

2 salmon fillets

Salt and pepper

¼ cup prepared pesto sauce

¼ cup diced tomatoes

STEAM | HIGH PRESSURE | 3 MINUTES | QUICK RELEASE

1. Pour 1 cup of water into the Instant Pot insert and drop in lemon wedges.

2. If your steam rack has very little solid surface area, place a piece of aluminum foil over it and poke many small holes to vent. Spray steam rack (with or without foil) with nonstick cooking spray.

3. Place salmon fillets on top of the steam rack and lightly season with salt and pepper.

4. Spread 2 tablespoons of pesto sauce over each salmon fillet.

5. Lower the steam rack with salmon into the insert in the cooker.

6. Secure lid and seal pressure release vent.

7. Set Instant Pot to STEAM on HIGH for 3 minutes.

8. Once cook time has elapsed, carefully perform a QUICK RELEASE of the pressure.

9. Serve salmon topped with diced tomatoes.

Make it My Way

If I have fresh basil on hand, I chop up a tablespoon or two and add it to the steaming liquid along with the lemon wedges. I also love to use this cooking method to make salmon spread with Italian or Caesar dressing in place of the pesto.

Just the Basics

This can be made with store-bought pesto, which you can find unrefrigerated in the pasta aisle or refrigerated near the fresh tortellini.

SEAFOOD

Notes

Cajun Shrimp Pasta

This creamy, Alfredo-like penne pasta dish has been made Cajun thanks to diced tomatoes, scallions, and a good amount of (somewhat spicy) Cajun seasoning. There's a surprisingly deep development of flavors for something that is truly toss and go, with no need to sauté any ingredients before cooking under pressure.

Ingredients

16 ounces penne pasta

4 cups chicken stock

1 (14.5-ounce) can diced tomatoes, with liquid

1 tablespoon Cajun seasoning

1 tablespoon minced garlic

1 pound large cooked and peeled shrimp (see Just the Basics)

³/₄ cup heavy cream

³/₄ cup grated Parmesan cheese

4 ounces cream cheese, chopped

¹/₄ cup sliced scallions

¹/₄ cup chopped fresh parsley

PRESSURE COOK | HIGH PRESSURE | 5 MINUTES | QUICK RELEASE

1 In the Instant Pot insert, stir to combine penne pasta, chicken stock, diced tomatoes, Cajun seasoning, and garlic.

2 Secure lid and seal pressure release vent.

3 Set Instant Pot to PRESSURE COOK on HIGH pressure for 5 minutes.

4 Once cook time has elapsed, carefully perform a QUICK RELEASE of the pressure.

5 Without draining any liquid, stir in shrimp, heavy cream, Parmesan cheese, cream cheese, and scallions.

6 Add additional Cajun seasoning to taste before serving topped with fresh parsley.

Make it My Way

For a complete meal, I usually serve this alongside a salad with peppercorn ranch dressing.

SEAFOOD

Just the Basics

Raw shrimp would overcook if cooked along with the pasta, so I usually use frozen cooked shrimp that are already peeled. I thaw them in the fridge overnight before using, but I've also run them under warm water to thaw.

Notes

Maryland Crab Dip

This hot party dip is like a Maryland crab boil on a chip—or whatever you choose to dip into it! It's an unexpected party dish that is equal parts upscale and comforting (I find that anything with cheese is automatically a comfort food).

Ingredients

12 ounces cream cheese, softened

1/3 cup mayonnaise

1/3 cup milk

2/3 cup grated Parmesan cheese

1 tablespoon minced garlic

1 tablespoon Worcestershire sauce

Juice of 1/2 lemon

2 teaspoons hot pepper sauce (such as Tabasco)

2 teaspoons Old Bay seasoning

2 teaspoons sugar

1 (12-ounce) can crab meat, drained

1/3 cup sliced scallions

Salt and pepper to taste

SLOW COOK | LESS | 90 MINUTES

1 In the Instant Pot insert, fold together cream cheese, mayonnaise, milk, Parmesan cheese, garlic, Worcestershire sauce, lemon juice, hot pepper sauce, Old Bay seasoning, and sugar.

2 Fold in crab meat and scallions.

3 Cover with a glass lid and set Instant Pot to SLOW COOK on LESS for 90 minutes, stirring halfway through cooking. Stir well after cooking.

4 Season with salt and pepper to taste before serving.

5 To serve at a party, set Instant Pot to KEEP WARM after cooking and stir every 30 minutes. If it cools down too much, simply switch to SLOW COOK on LESS.

Make it My Way

Plain pita chips are great for dipping into this dip. Crisp celery is also particularly good!

Just the Basics

Any variety of canned crab meat will work in this recipe, as will refrigerated crab meat sold in small containers in the fresh seafood section of the grocery store.

SEAFOOD

Notes _____

Shrimp Scampi

While cooking under pressure is a standout feature of the Instant Pot, I find myself using it more and more for simpler tasks like sautéing. I find the results very predictable and the cleanup a breeze. When it comes to seafood and sautéing, there's nothing simpler than the classic Shrimp Scampi.

Ingredients

¼ cup butter, divided

2 tablespoons olive oil

1½ pounds large shrimp, peeled

2 tablespoons minced garlic

¼ teaspoon salt

¼ teaspoon pepper

¼ cup dry white wine

Juice of ½ lemon

¼ cup chopped fresh parsley

SAUTÉ | 10 MINUTES

1 Preheat the Instant Pot insert on SAUTÉ. Add 2 tablespoons of the butter and all of the olive oil and heat until sizzling hot.

2 Add shrimp and garlic and season with the salt and pepper.

3 Sauté for 3 minutes before pouring in the wine and lemon juice.

4 Bring up to a simmer and let cook 2 minutes or just until shrimp are pink and opaque throughout.

5 Turn off heat and stir in the remaining 2 tablespoons of butter.

6 Adjust salt and pepper to taste before serving topped with fresh parsley.

Make it My Way

When I make this to serve over pasta, I sometimes stir in a little extra butter at the end for even more sauce to drizzle over the pasta.

SEAFOOD

Just the Basics

Chicken stock, ½ teaspoon of sugar, and juice of the other ½ of the lemon can be used in place of the white wine, if desired.

Notes

Fish with Capers and Dill

Many home cooks are intimidated by seafood, especially fish, as there is such a brief window between perfectly cooked and overcooked. Poaching cod or salmon sous vide removes any of the guesswork and ensures a perfect piece of fish that practically cooks itself.

Ingredients

- 2 skinless cod or salmon fillets (5–8 ounces each)
- Salt and pepper
- 2 sprigs fresh dill
- 4 thin slices lemon
- 1 tablespoon butter, melted
- 1 tablespoon extra-virgin olive oil
- 2 teaspoons capers, drained

SOUS VIDE | 130°F | 1 HOUR

1. Place steam rack at the bottom of the Instant Pot insert and fill the insert with water to the MAX line. Place lid on Instant Pot.

2. Set Instant Pot to SOUS VIDE at 130°F for medium (very moist) or 140°F for well done (very flaky). Set the cook time to 1 hour.

3. Lightly season each fish fillet with salt and pepper and then top with a whole sprig of dill and 2 slices of lemon.

4. Place fillets in a vacuum-seal bag in a single layer and pour in butter and olive oil. Add capers and seal bag.

5. Once water temperature is reached, submerge the bag in the water, secure lid on Instant Pot, and vent pressure valve to remain open. You may also cover with a glass lid.

6. Once cook time has elapsed, remove fish and serve drizzled with the capers and cooking liquid inside the bag.

Make it My Way

I like to serve this with the whole sprigs of dill and whole slices of lemon over top as it makes for a nice presentation, but you also can chop the dill and add 2 teaspoons of lemon juice to the bag before cooking instead.

SEAFOOD

Just the Basics

Be sure to buy skinless fish fillets, as this is simply poached and not seared, so the skin will not be crisped up.

Notes

Teriyaki Salmon

Using the sous vide function on the Instant Pot will allow you to perfectly cook salmon to restaurant standards every time. This recipe infuses the fish with an Asian teriyaki glaze, but you could use the same directions to prepare salmon with just a splash of lemon juice, salt, pepper, and chopped fresh dill for more traditional flavors. This recipe also can be easily doubled to make 4 fillets.

Ingredients

2 salmon fillets (5–8 ounces each), brined (see Just the Basics below)

¼ cup teriyaki marinade and glaze

1 teaspoon grated fresh ginger

Zest of ½ orange

1 tablespoon vegetable oil, optional

1 tablespoon sesame oil, optional

SOUS VIDE | 130°F | 1 HOUR

1 Place steam rack at the bottom of the Instant Pot insert and fill the insert with water to the MAX line. Place lid on Instant Pot.

2 Set Instant Pot to SOUS VIDE at 130°F for medium (very moist) or 140°F for well done (very flaky). Set the cook time to 1 hour.

3 For the best results, place each salmon fillet in an individual vacuum-seal bag, or they may bond to each other and cook into one large fillet.

4 In a small bowl, whisk together teriyaki marinade, ginger, and orange zest. Spoon 1 tablespoon of this mixture into each vacuum-seal bag. Reserve remaining marinade for after cooking.

5 Seal vacuum bags. Once water temperature is reached, submerge the bags in the water, secure lid on Instant Pot, and vent pressure valve to remain open. You may also cover with a glass lid.

6 Once cook time has elapsed, carefully remove salmon from bags. Salmon can be served immediately by drizzling with the reserved marinade.

7 For better flavor, pat salmon dry with paper towels. Drain Instant Pot insert and set to SAUTÉ. Allow at least 2 minutes to preheat before adding vegetable oil and sesame oil and heating at least 30 seconds.

8 Sear the cooked salmon on at least 1 side (the skin side if the fillets have skin). Turn off cooker and pour the remaining marinade over the salmon, flipping once, before serving.

Just the Basics

For the best-looking salmon, soak it in a bowl of 2 cups water and 2 tablespoons kosher salt for at least 30 minutes before cooking. Rinse well. This helps reduce the (admittedly harmless) white protein called "albumen" that cooks out of the fish.

SEAFOOD

Notes

Meatless Mains

pressure cook

MEATLESS

Vegetarian Stuffed Peppers

Whole peppers are stuffed with brown rice and veggie (ground-beef style) crumbles in this colorful dish that you cook right inside the serving "dish"—a whole bell pepper.

Ingredients

2 large bell peppers (any color)

1 cup cooked brown rice

3/4 cup frozen veggie crumbles

1/2 cup diced tomatoes with green chilies (Rotel)

1/2 cup canned chickpeas, drained

1 tablespoon chopped fresh oregano

1 1/2 teaspoons minced garlic

1 teaspoon light brown sugar

1/4 teaspoon salt

1/8 teaspoon pepper

STEAM | HIGH PRESSURE | 4 MINUTES | NATURAL RELEASE

1. Place a steam rack in the Instant Pot insert and pour in 1 cup of water.

2. Slice the tops off the bell peppers and discard or set aside for a better presentation when serving. Scoop out all seeds and white flesh inside the peppers and discard.

3. In a mixing bowl, fold together all remaining ingredients to make the filling.

4. Spoon the filling evenly into both peppers and press down to pack it tightly. Place the stuffed peppers on the steam rack in the insert.

5. Secure lid and seal pressure release vent.

6. Set Instant Pot to STEAM on HIGH for 4 minutes.

7. Once cook time has elapsed, let the pressure release through NATURAL RELEASE for 5 minutes before carefully quick releasing any remaining pressure.

8. Carefully remove peppers from the pot using silicone tongs and serve immediately.

Make it My Way

I make this using a pouch of precooked brown "Ready Rice," but you also can make it with frozen cooked brown rice.

Just the Basics

An alternative to ground beef, the veggie crumbles used in this recipe are sold in the frozen veggie burger section of the grocery store.

Notes

_____

_____

MEATLESS

Meat-Free Chili Mac

Elbow macaroni is infused with the flavors of chili as this hearty vegetarian dish cooks under pressure. What really takes it to the next level is cheese—both Cheddar cheese and cream cheese—which complements both the chili and the macaroni.

Ingredients

1 tablespoon vegetable oil

1 small yellow onion, diced

1 small green bell pepper, diced

2 tablespoons chili powder

1 tablespoon minced garlic

2 teaspoons ground cumin

3 ¾ cups vegetable stock

16 ounces elbow macaroni

2 (15-ounce) cans dark red kidney beans, drained

½ teaspoon salt

¼ teaspoon pepper

1 (8-ounce) can tomato sauce

2 tablespoons tomato paste

2 teaspoons sugar

4 ounces cream cheese, chopped

1 ½ cups sharp Cheddar cheese

PRESSURE COOK | HIGH PRESSURE | 5 MINUTES | QUICK RELEASE

1 Preheat the Instant Pot insert on SAUTÉ. Add vegetable oil and heat until it thins out.

2 Add onion, bell pepper, chili powder, garlic, and cumin and sauté for 3 minutes, just until onion begins to turn translucent.

3 Pour in vegetable stock and deglaze the insert before stirring in macaroni, kidney beans, salt, and pepper.

4 Top with tomato sauce, tomato paste, and sugar but do not stir into the other ingredients. Secure lid and seal pressure release vent.

5 Set Instant Pot to PRESSURE COOK on HIGH pressure for 5 minutes.

6 Once cook time has elapsed, carefully perform a QUICK RELEASE of the pressure.

7 Without draining any liquid, stir in cream cheese and Cheddar cheese. Let stand 3 minutes to thicken before serving.

Just the Basics

You also can make this with 8 ounces of processed cheese (Velveeta) in place of both the cream cheese and Cheddar cheese.

Notes _____

_____

MEATLESS

Ratatouille

Many people wouldn't think of stewed vegetables as a main dish; but when you serve this French classic over rice, you have a hearty meal full of well-developed flavors.

Ingredients

3 tablespoons olive oil

1 red onion, chopped

1 red bell pepper, chopped

2 tablespoons minced garlic

2 teaspoons Italian seasoning

1/3 cup vegetable stock

1 eggplant, chopped into 1-inch pieces

2 zucchini, chopped into 1-inch pieces

1 (28-ounce) can whole peeled tomatoes, drained

1/4 cup chopped fresh basil

1 tablespoon balsamic vinegar

1 teaspoon sugar

1/4 teaspoon salt

1/4 teaspoon pepper

PRESSURE COOK | HIGH PRESSURE | 4 MINUTES | QUICK RELEASE

1 Preheat the Instant Pot insert on SAUTÉ. Add olive oil and heat until it thins out.

2 Add onion, bell pepper, garlic, and Italian seasoning and sauté for 4 minutes, just until onion begins to turn translucent.

3 Pour in vegetable stock and deglaze the insert before stirring in all remaining ingredients.

4 Secure lid and seal pressure release vent.

5 Set Instant Pot to PRESSURE COOK on HIGH pressure for 4 minutes.

6 Once cook time has elapsed, carefully perform a QUICK RELEASE of the pressure.

7 Adjust seasoning with sugar, salt, and pepper to taste before serving.

MEATLESS

Just the Basics

Make this into even more of a full and satisfying meal by serving topped with fried or poached eggs.

Notes

Superfood Farro Salad

ⓥ

This vibrant, vegetarian salad is filled with nutrient-dense foods that look and taste great. Farro is a grain that is loaded with fiber, protein, vitamins, minerals, and antioxidants. Served warm, this is topped with sweet mandarin oranges and pomegranate seeds but is primarily a savory dish, which is particularly great when served around the holidays.

Ingredients

1 cup pearled farro, rinsed

1³/₄ cups vegetable stock

1 sprig fresh rosemary

2 tablespoons extra-virgin olive oil, divided

6 packed cups chopped kale

1 tablespoon balsamic vinegar

Salt and pepper to taste

1 cup mandarin oranges, drained

¹/₃ cup pomegranate seeds

¹/₄ cup toasted sliced almonds

BEAN/GRAIN | HIGH PRESSURE | 10 MINUTES | NATURAL RELEASE

1 In the Instant Pot insert, stir to combine farro, vegetable stock, rosemary, and 1 tablespoon of the olive oil.

2 Secure lid and seal pressure release vent.

3 Set Instant Pot to BEAN/GRAIN or PRESSURE COOK on HIGH pressure for 10 minutes.

4 Once cook time has elapsed, let the pressure release through NATURAL RELEASE.

5 Stir in kale, cover, and let stand 3 minutes to gently cook the kale (it will still be crisp).

6 Stir in balsamic vinegar and season with salt and pepper to taste.

7 Serve topped with mandarin oranges, pomegranate seeds, and sliced almonds.

Make it My Way

While there are a lot of sweet ingredients in this dish, I still find the farro to be very savory in a way that complements them well. In fact, I like to add a small drizzle of honey to the farro to balance things out even further.

MEATLESS

Just the Basics

Farro is a robust grain in the wheat family, which is similar to barley in taste and texture.

Notes

Mediterranean Quinoa

High-protein quinoa makes this dish satisfying, whether served as a side or even a full vegetarian meal. It's packed with the Mediterranean flavors of garlic, oregano, lemon, tomato, kalamata olive, and feta cheese.

Ingredients

1½ cups quinoa

1½ cups vegetable stock

2 tablespoons extra-virgin olive oil, divided

1 tablespoon chopped fresh oregano

2 teaspoons minced garlic

2 teaspoons light brown sugar

1 teaspoon lemon zest

1 tomato, diced

⅓ cup chopped kalamata olives

⅓ cup crumbled feta cheese

Salt and pepper to taste

BEAN/GRAIN | HIGH PRESSURE | 1 MINUTE | NATURAL RELEASE

1. In the Instant Pot insert, stir to combine quinoa, vegetable stock, 1 tablespoon of the olive oil, oregano, garlic, brown sugar, and lemon zest.

2. Secure lid and seal pressure release vent.

3. Set Instant Pot to BEAN/GRAIN or PRESSURE COOK on HIGH pressure for 1 minute.

4. Once cook time has elapsed, let the pressure release through NATURAL RELEASE.

5. Fluff quinoa with a fork and stir in tomato, kalamata olives, feta cheese, and remaining tablespoon of olive oil. Season with salt and pepper to taste before serving.

Make it My Way

You can use a cup of cherry or grape tomatoes (halved) in place of the regular diced tomatoes. I find them much easier to work with and can look really nice if you buy the multicolored variety.

MEATLESS

Just the Basics

Many people suggest rinsing quinoa to "reduce bitterness," but most quinoa sold now is prerinsed and not bitter at all. Rinsing it is not only a pain but can leave the results a bit mushy for my liking. I say skip the rinse!

Notes —

Lentil Sloppy Joes

Lentils make the perfect substitute for ground meat in this vegan (depending on the hamburger buns you buy) take on Sloppy Joe sandwiches. When you think about it, what makes a Sloppy Joe a Sloppy Joe is a sweet and savory barbecue sauce and lots of it, not the flavor of the meat within that sauce, so it makes a lot of sense that you can recreate the filling in a plant-based way without sacrificing flavor.

Ingredients

1 tablespoon olive oil

1 small yellow onion, diced

1 carrot, diced

2 teaspoons minced garlic

2 teaspoons smoked paprika

1/4 teaspoon allspice

2 1/4 cups water

1 cup lentils, rinsed

2 tablespoons dark brown sugar

2 tablespoons yellow mustard

1 teaspoon Worcestershire sauce

1/2 teaspoon onion powder

1/4 cup barbecue sauce

1/4 cup ketchup

Salt and pepper to taste

Hamburger buns, to serve

BEAN/GRAIN | HIGH PRESSURE | 15 MINUTES | NATURAL RELEASE

1 Preheat the Instant Pot insert on SAUTÉ. Add olive oil and heat until it thins out.

2 Add onion, carrot, garlic, smoked paprika, and allspice and sauté for 3 minutes, just until onion begins to turn translucent.

3 Pour in water and deglaze the insert before stirring in lentils, brown sugar, yellow mustard, Worcestershire sauce, and onion powder.

4 Secure lid and seal pressure release vent.

5 Set Instant Pot to BEAN/GRAIN on HIGH pressure for 15 minutes.

6 Once cook time has elapsed, let the pressure release through NATURAL RELEASE.

7 Stir in barbecue sauce and ketchup before seasoning with salt and pepper to taste.

8 Serve on hamburger buns with your favorite fixings.

Make it My Way

Top your Sloppy Joes with any combination of pickles, sliced red onion, Cheddar cheese, lettuce and tomato, or my personal favorite: coleslaw.

Just the Basics

Traditional Sloppy Joes are typically very, very sweet, so feel free to add additional brown sugar to taste as you season with salt and pepper.

MEATLESS

Notes

Quinoa Chili

Quinoa is super high in protein which makes it perfect to use in place of ground beef in this vegan chili. It may seem strange at first, but I promise that the results are delicious and make a lot more sense when you consider that quinoa has the protein of beef and the (whole grain) carbohydrates of rice that you would serve alongside a traditional chili.

Ingredients

1 tablespoon olive oil

1 cup diced red onion

½ cup diced red bell pepper

1½ tablespoons chili powder

1 tablespoon minced garlic

2 teaspoons ground cumin

2½ cups vegetable stock

1¼ cups quinoa

1 (15-ounce) can black beans, drained

1 (14.5-ounce) can diced tomatoes, with liquid

¾ cup frozen corn

¼ cup chopped fresh cilantro

1 tablespoon sugar

1 cup chunky salsa

Salt and pepper to taste

Chopped avocado, for garnish

BEAN/GRAIN | HIGH PRESSURE | 2 MINUTES | NATURAL RELEASE

1 Preheat the Instant Pot insert on SAUTÉ. Add olive oil and heat until it thins out.

2 Add onion, bell pepper, chili powder, garlic, and cumin and sauté for 3 minutes, just until onion begins to turn translucent.

3 Pour in vegetable stock and deglaze the insert before stirring in quinoa, black beans, diced tomatoes, corn, cilantro, and sugar.

4 Secure lid and seal pressure release vent.

5 Set Instant Pot to BEAN/GRAIN on HIGH pressure for 2 minutes.

6 Once cook time has elapsed, let the pressure release through NATURAL RELEASE.

7 Stir in salsa and season with salt and pepper to taste before serving topped with chopped avocado, if desired.

MEATLESS

Just the Basics

Quinoa loves to absorb liquid. If the chili is too thin, simply set to SAUTÉ and simmer, stirring constantly, until your desired consistency. If it is too thick, add additional vegetable stock or salsa.

Notes

Red Bean and Spanish Rice Burritos

The Spanish rice in these burritos is so good that it deserves to be its own recipe. You can prepare it without stuffing it into a burrito, but these burritos are where the rice truly shines. While they are only made with a few ingredients (after preparing the rice), these ingredients all balance each other out and truly make for the perfect bite.

Ingredients

2 tablespoons olive oil

3/4 cup diced yellow onion

1/2 cup diced green bell pepper

1 tablespoon chili powder

2 teaspoons minced garlic

1 1/2 teaspoons ground cumin

1/4 teaspoon salt

1/4 teaspoon pepper

1 1/4 cups vegetable stock

1 1/4 cups long grain white rice, rinsed

1/3 cup petite diced tomatoes, drained

1 (15-ounce) can red beans, drained

4 large flour tortillas

3/4 cup guacamole

RICE | HIGH PRESSURE | LESS | NATURAL RELEASE

1 Preheat the Instant Pot insert on SAUTÉ. Add olive oil and heat until the oil thins out.

2 Add onion, bell pepper, chili powder, garlic, cumin, salt, and pepper and sauté for 3 minutes or until onion is translucent.

3 Pour in vegetable stock and deglaze the insert before stirring in rice and tomatoes.

4 Secure lid and seal pressure release vent.

5 Set Instant Pot to RICE on HIGH pressure on the LESS preset.

6 Once cook time has elapsed, let the pressure release through NATURAL RELEASE for 10 minutes before quick releasing any remaining pressure.

7 Meanwhile, warm the red beans by microwaving for 1–2 minutes, just until hot.

8 Assemble 4 burritos by spooning about 2/3 cup of the rice atop each of the flour tortillas. Top each with about 1/3 cup of the beans and a few tablespoons of guacamole.

9 Fold the ends of the tortillas in as you roll everything up into finished burritos.

MEATLESS

Just the Basics

Serve this drizzled with picante or taco sauce over top or on the side for dipping.

Notes

Vegetables and Sides

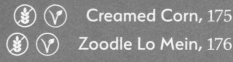

SIDES

157

Roasted Baby Potatoes

Baby potatoes cook under pressure to create a nice creamy texture inside before sautéing to form a crispy and browned skin outside. Rosemary and garlic are added to the steaming liquid to infuse more flavor into the potatoes as they cook.

Ingredients

1 cup water or chicken stock

2 sprigs fresh rosemary

3 cloves garlic

24 ounces baby gold or multicolored potatoes

2 tablespoons olive oil

1 tablespoon butter

Salt and pepper

Garlic powder

3 tablespoons grated Parmesan cheese

2 tablespoons chopped fresh parsley

ACCESSORIES

Steam basket

STEAM | HIGH PRESSURE | 8 MINUTES | QUICK RELEASE

1 Pour 1 cup of water into the Instant Pot insert and then lower steam basket into the pot. Add rosemary and garlic.

2 Rinse and pierce the potatoes with a fork to prevent them from splitting under pressure. Transfer to the steam basket inside the pot.

3 Secure lid and seal pressure release vent.

4 Set Instant Pot to STEAM on HIGH pressure for 8 minutes.

5 Once cook time has elapsed, carefully perform a QUICK RELEASE of the pressure.

6 Remove steam basket and drain all cooking liquid from the insert. Discard rosemary and garlic.

7 Preheat the Instant Pot insert on SAUTÉ. Add olive oil and butter and heat until butter is sizzling.

8 Place the cooked potatoes in the pot and lightly season with salt, pepper, and garlic powder.

9 Gently toss the potatoes to rotate every minute, until most potatoes are browned on a few sides. Transfer to a serving dish and toss in Parmesan cheese and parsley before serving.

Just the Basics

Adding the aromatics of rosemary and garlic to the cooking liquid really infuses the potatoes with flavor, but they can be skipped if you'd like to shorten your shopping list.

SIDES

Notes

Maple Bacon Brussels Sprouts

My mom used to make brussels sprouts when I was growing up, but I never ate them! I also never cooked them in my home . . . until recently. Cooking them with veggie stock, bacon, and maple syrup has absolutely changed the way I feel about brussels sprouts!

Ingredients

1 cup vegetable stock

1 pound brussels sprouts, halved

¼ cup pure maple syrup, divided

1 tablespoon butter

6 slices bacon, chopped

½ cup diced yellow onion

Salt and pepper to taste

ACCESSORIES

Steam basket

STEAM | HIGH PRESSURE | 2 MINUTES | QUICK RELEASE

1 Pour vegetable stock into the Instant Pot insert and then lower steam basket into the pot.

2 Fill the steam basket with the brussels sprouts and drizzle with ½ of the maple syrup.

3 Secure lid and seal pressure release vent. Set Instant Pot to STEAM on HIGH pressure for 2 minutes.

4 Once cook time has elapsed, carefully perform a QUICK RELEASE of the pressure.

5 Immediately remove steam basket and set aside. Drain insert well.

6 Preheat the Instant Pot insert on SAUTÉ. Add butter and heat until sizzling.

7 Add the bacon and cook until nearly crisp and then drain at least ½ of the grease.

8 Add onion and sauté 3 minutes. Stir in cooked brussels sprouts and the remaining maple syrup and sauté 1 minute. Season with salt and pepper to taste before serving.

Just the Basics

If your brussels sprouts are on the smaller size (around the size of a quarter) you should keep them whole. Unusually large brussels sprouts that are approaching the size of a baby potato (it happens) should be quartered.

SIDES

Notes

Steamed Broccoli or Cauliflower

Broccoli and/or cauliflower are likely the most delicate things you can cook in an Instant Pot. It is absolutely crucial that you use a steam basket to keep them above the cooking liquid and perform a quick release of the pressure as soon as the cook time has elapsed. I always get the best results by cutting large florets and arranging the naturally smaller florets toward the top of the steam basket.

Ingredients

1 bunch broccoli or 1 head cauliflower, cut into large florets

1 cup chicken or vegetable stock

2 cloves garlic, optional

3 tablespoons butter, optional

Salt and pepper to taste

ACCESSORIES

Steam basket

Just the Basics

If your florets are large, you may want to cook them for 1 minute. If 1 minute is not enough, try cooking for another minute. (This is why I have a place for notes at the bottom of each page. Jot down a note with the perfect time for you.) Also, never leave steamed veggies in the pot for long; they overcook quickly! For frozen broccoli or cauliflower, increase the cook time to 2 minutes.

STEAM | HIGH PRESSURE | 1 MINUTE | QUICK RELEASE

1 Fill steam basket with broccoli, cauliflower, or a mixture of both.

2 Pour chicken or vegetable stock into the Instant Pot insert and then add garlic cloves, if desired.

3 Lower steam basket into the insert.

4 Secure lid and seal pressure release vent.

5 Set Instant Pot to STEAM on HIGH pressure for 0 minutes for crisp-tender and 1 minute for entirely tender. By setting to 0 minutes the Instant Pot will slowly come up to pressure and then turn off.

6 Once cook time has elapsed, carefully perform a QUICK RELEASE of the pressure.

7 Remove steam basket immediately and top vegetables with butter, if desired. Season with salt and pepper to taste.

Make it My Way

I like to season both broccoli and cauliflower with grated Parmesan cheese. Toss the cooked vegetables in $\frac{1}{4}$ cup of Parmesan cheese while they're still hot, right out of the Instant Pot.

SIDES

Notes

Sour Cream and Chive Mashed Potatoes

There's no need to worry about the water boiling over when preparing potatoes in the Instant Pot. You also get the great benefit of being able to infuse flavor directly into the potatoes as they cook. In this instance, I simply use onion powder while cooking to enhance the flavor of the chives that are added after mashing.

Ingredients

3 pounds Russet or Yukon Gold potatoes, peeled and cut into large pieces

3/4 teaspoon salt

1/2 teaspoon onion powder

1/2 cup sour cream

3 tablespoons butter

2 tablespoons grated Parmesan cheese

2 tablespoons chopped chives

Salt and pepper to taste

PRESSURE COOK | HIGH PRESSURE | 6 MINUTES | QUICK RELEASE

1 Place potato pieces in the Instant Pot insert and fill with enough water to cover the potatoes. Stir in salt and onion powder.

2 Secure lid and seal pressure release vent.

3 Set Instant Pot to PRESSURE COOK on HIGH pressure for 6 minutes.

4 Once cook time has elapsed, carefully perform a QUICK RELEASE of the pressure.

5 Fully drain potatoes and return to the pot.

6 With a potato masher, mash the sour cream, butter, and Parmesan cheese into the potatoes. Mash until they've reached your desired consistency. For a thinner mash, add a few tablespoons of milk or warm water.

7 Fold in chopped chives and season with salt and pepper to taste before serving.

Make it My Way

For even more flavor, I sometimes cook my potatoes in chicken stock or a mixture of chicken stock and water.

SIDES

Just the Basics

Hand mashing is always the best way to go, as using a blender or food processor will make the final result sticky like glue.

Notes

Cheesy Potatoes Au Gratin

Au Gratin Potatoes can take as long as 2 hours when made from raw potatoes in the oven. Sometimes they just cook and cook and never seem to get tender! This recipe steams sliced potatoes in the Instant Pot in 2 minutes under pressure before assembling the casserole to simply brown the cheese in the oven.

Ingredients

2 pounds Russet or Yukon Gold potatoes

1/2 cup diced yellow onion

1 1/4 cups chicken or vegetable stock

1/2 cup heavy cream

1 tablespoon cornstarch

2 tablespoons water

2 cups shredded Colby-Jack cheese, divided

Salt and pepper to taste

Chopped chives, for garnish

ACCESSORIES

Steam basket

STEAM | HIGH PRESSURE | 2 MINUTES | QUICK RELEASE

1 Peel and slice potatoes into 1/4-inch-thick slices. Do not slice too thin! Transfer to a steam basket. Top with the diced onion and lower into the Instant Pot insert.

2 Pour the stock into the insert. Secure lid and seal pressure release vent.

3 Set Instant Pot to STEAM on HIGH pressure for 2 minutes.

4 Once the cooker has come up to pressure and turned off, carefully perform a QUICK RELEASE of the pressure.

5 Immediately remove steam basket of potatoes from the insert and transfer potatoes to a 2-quart or 8-inch square baking dish.

6 Set Instant Pot to SAUTÉ and stir heavy cream into the potato cooking liquid. Bring up to a simmer.

7 Whisk cornstarch into 2 tablespoons of water and stir into the simmering liquid. Let cook 1 minute, just until thickened. Turn off heat and stir in 1 1/2 cups of the Colby-Jack cheese. Season sauce with salt and pepper to taste.

8 Pour the sauce over the potatoes in the baking dish and top with the remaining 1/2 cup of Colby-Jack cheese.

9 Broil for 5 minutes or until lightly browned and bubbly hot. For baking dishes that are not broiler safe, bake at 400°F for 15 minutes or until bubbly hot. Sprinkle with chives.

Just the Basics

Instant Pot is releasing a new Air Fryer Lid that can make this recipe even simpler. Simply stir the potatoes into the cheese sauce in the insert and top with remaining cheese. Lock on Air Fryer Lid, set to BROIL, and cook until lightly browned, about 4 minutes.

SIDES

Notes

Fried Apples

While they taste like dessert, Fried Apples are a classic Southern side dish, which goes especially well with pork or picnic dishes.

Ingredients

4 large Granny Smith apples

2 teaspoons lemon juice

1/3 cup water

2/3 cup dark brown sugar, divided

2 teaspoons ground cinnamon

1/4 teaspoon vanilla extract

Pinch nutmeg

Pinch salt

1 tablespoon cornstarch

2 tablespoons water

PRESSURE COOK | HIGH PRESSURE | 4 MINUTES | QUICK RELEASE

1 Toss apples in lemon juice as you core and cut them into wedges, leaving the peel on.

2 Transfer the apple wedges to the Instant Pot insert and add water, 1/2 of the brown sugar, cinnamon, vanilla extract, nutmeg, and salt. Toss to combine.

3 Secure lid and seal pressure release vent.

4 Set Instant Pot to PRESSURE COOK on HIGH for 4 minutes.

5 Once cook time has elapsed, place a kitchen towel over the steam vent (it could splatter hot sugar) and QUICK RELEASE the pressure.

6 Set Instant Pot to SAUTÉ and stir in the remaining brown sugar. Bring up to a simmer.

7 Whisk the cornstarch into 2 tablespoons of water and then stir into the apples, bringing back up to a simmer for 1 minute, just until thickened. Serve warm.

Make it My Way

I also like to make this with a mix of 2 Granny Smith apples and 2 sweet Honeycrisp apples for a little variety in flavor.

Just the Basics

Leaving the peel on the apple wedges helps them hold their shape as they cook up tender; otherwise, you may end up halfway to making applesauce.

SIDES

Notes

Quick and Easy Potato Salad

Potato salad has never been easier than this! Hard-boiled eggs are steamed right over top of the chopped potatoes for a classic picnic staple made in only one pot.

Ingredients

3 pounds Russet or Yukon
  Gold potatoes

3 large eggs

1 cup mayonnaise

3 tablespoons minced
  yellow onion

1½ tablespoons sweet relish

1½ tablespoons yellow mustard

1 tablespoon chopped
  fresh parsley

Salt and pepper to taste

ACCESSORIES

Steam basket

STEAM | HIGH PRESSURE | 4 MINUTES | QUICK RELEASE

1 Peel and chop potatoes into large pieces (about 1 inch). Transfer to a steam basket. Top with the eggs, in the shell.

2 Pour 1 cup of water into the Instant Pot insert and then lower steam basket into the pot.

3 Secure lid and seal pressure release vent.

4 Set Instant Pot to STEAM on HIGH pressure for 4 minutes.

5 Once cook time has elapsed, carefully perform a QUICK RELEASE of the pressure.

6 Remove steam basket, transfer eggs to a bath of ice water, and run potatoes under cold running water for 1 minute.

7 Once cooled, peel and chop the eggs.

8 In a mixing bowl, stir together mayonnaise, onion, relish, mustard, and parsley to create a dressing.

9 Gently fold the cooled potatoes and chopped eggs into the dressing and season with salt and pepper to taste. For best flavor, cover and refrigerate at least 2 hours before serving.

Just the Basics

The larger you cut the potatoes, the firmer they will be in the finished salad; however, anything under 1-inch may come out too soft to fully hold together.

SIDES

Notes

Simply Spaghetti Squash

Pasta is probably my favorite food, but it's always nice to cut back on carbohydrates and eat lighter for a day or two a week. Spaghetti squash is a really great way to do that, as it can be served in many of the same ways that you'd serve ordinary spaghetti. This was an entirely new food to me when I first got my Instant Pot, but I now love it! I will often sprinkle the squash with garlic powder before cooking under pressure.

Ingredients

1 medium (2-pound) spaghetti squash

2 tablespoons butter, optional

Chopped parsley, optional

Salt and pepper to taste

STEAM | HIGH PRESSURE | 7 MINUTES | QUICK RELEASE

1 Place a steam rack in Instant Pot insert and pour in 1 cup of water.

2 Using a heavy knife, cut spaghetti squash in half lengthwise.

3 Scoop out seeds and fibrous pulp in the center of each half and discard pulp. The seeds can be roasted like pumpkin seeds (see below).

4 Place both squash halves atop the steam rack in the Instant Pot. You may have to angle them up against the walls of the insert to get them to fit.

5 Secure lid and seal pressure release vent.

6 Set Instant Pot to STEAM on HIGH pressure for 7 minutes.

7 Once cook time has elapsed, carefully perform a QUICK RELEASE of the pressure.

8 I like to place a tablespoon of butter in each cooked half, letting it melt into the squash before topping with parsley and seasoning with salt and pepper to taste. To serve, use two forks to pull spaghetti-like strands from the squash.

Just the Basics

Cutting the squash in half can be a tricky job, but it can be made easier by using a large serrated knife. I also find that placing it in a bed made out of a large kitchen towel will help hold it in place as you cut.

Roasting Seeds

Toss in 2 teaspoons of olive oil and season lightly with salt. Spread out on a sheet pan lined with parchment paper. Cook at 300°F for 25 minutes, stirring halfway through, just until golden brown.

SIDES

Notes

Mashed Sweet Potato Casserole

These mashed sweet potatoes are made into a take on sweet potato casserole by swirling marshmallow fluff into the top and sprinkling with crunchy pecans. For a more savory sweet potato mash, without the marshmallow, see "Just the Basics" below, but why wouldn't you want marshmallow!?

Ingredients

2 pounds sweet potatoes, peeled and chopped into 1-inch pieces

¼ cup pure maple syrup

¼ teaspoon ground cinnamon

3 tablespoons butter

1 tablespoon brown sugar

¼ teaspoon salt

¾ cup marshmallow fluff

½ cup chopped pecans

ACCESSORIES

Steam basket

STEAM | HIGH PRESSURE | 7 MINUTES | QUICK RELEASE

1 Pour 1 cup of water into the Instant Pot insert and then lower steam basket into the insert.

2 Place chopped sweet potatoes in the steam basket in the insert and drizzle with maple syrup. Sprinkle with ground cinnamon.

3 Secure lid and seal pressure release vent.

4 Set Instant Pot to STEAM on HIGH pressure for 7 minutes.

5 Once cook time has elapsed, carefully perform a QUICK RELEASE of the pressure.

6 Remove steam basket and drain insert. Transfer cooked sweet potatoes into the empty insert.

7 Fully drain potatoes and return to the pot.

8 With a potato masher, mash the butter, brown sugar, and salt into the potatoes. Mash until they've reached your desired consistency.

9 Transfer to a serving dish and top with the marshmallow fluff, lightly swirling it into the potatoes. Top with chopped pecans and serve immediately.

Make it My Way

If you get Instant Pot's new Air Fryer Lid, you can top this with whole marshmallows and set to BROIL to brown them right in the pot!

Just the Basics

For more savory mashed sweet potatoes, steam in chicken stock with 4 fresh sage leaves. Omit the brown sugar when mashing and skip the marshmallow fluff topping.

SIDES

Notes

Boston Baked Beans

This is my mother's classic recipe for Boston Baked Beans with only one big change: It no longer takes six hours of baking in a hot oven! With sweet molasses and savory salt pork, it's everything you want in homemade baked beans in a whole lot less time.

Ingredients

2 tablespoons olive oil

1 cup chopped salt pork

1 medium white onion, chopped

6 cups water

1 pound dried navy beans, sorted and rinsed

$\frac{1}{2}$ cup molasses

$\frac{1}{2}$ cup dark brown sugar

1 teaspoon salt

$\frac{1}{2}$ teaspoon ground mustard

$\frac{1}{4}$ teaspoon pepper

BEAN/GRAIN | HIGH PRESSURE | 60 MINUTES | NATURAL RELEASE

1. Preheat the Instant Pot insert on SAUTÉ. Add olive oil and heat until it thins out.

2. Add salt pork and onion and sauté until pork begins to brown.

3. Pour in water and deglaze the insert before stirring in beans and all remaining ingredients.

4. Secure lid and seal pressure release vent.

5. Set Instant Pot to BEAN/GRAIN or PRESSURE COOK on HIGH pressure for 60 minutes.

6. Once cook time has elapsed, let the pressure release through NATURAL RELEASE.

7. For a thicker consistency, set the Instant Pot to SAUTÉ and let simmer until the beans have thickened to your liking.

Make it My Way

I like to make these with the traditional salt pork; however, 8 strips of bacon (chopped) can be substituted in its place.

SIDES

Just the Basics

Always sort and rinse dried beans to discard any irregularly shaped beans, as those may actually be small stones.

Notes

Green Beans Almondine

These green beans are flash-steamed under pressure (in so little time that you have to set the Instant Pot to 0 minutes) and finished by sautéing in butter and garlic. Slivered almonds add a nutty crunch that finishes out a classic side dish.

Ingredients

1 pound green beans, ends snapped

1 cup vegetable stock

2 tablespoons butter

1 tablespoon vegetable oil

1/3 cup finely diced yellow onion

1 tablespoon minced garlic

1/2 cup slivered almonds

Salt and pepper to taste

ACCESSORIES

Steam basket

STEAM | LOW PRESSURE | 0 MINUTES | QUICK RELEASE

1 Fill steam basket with green beans and then lower steam basket into the Instant Pot insert. Pour in vegetable stock.

2 Secure lid and seal pressure release vent.

3 Set Instant Pot to STEAM on LOW pressure for 0 minutes. By setting to 0 minutes the Instant Pot will slowly come up to pressure and then turn off.

4 Once the cooker has come up to pressure and turned off, carefully perform a QUICK RELEASE of the pressure.

5 Remove steam basket, set aside, and drain insert before returning it to the cooker.

6 Preheat the Instant Pot insert on SAUTÉ. Add butter and vegetable oil and heat until sizzling.

7 Add onion and garlic and sauté 3 minutes, just until onion is translucent.

8 Add slivered almonds and steamed green beans and sauté 1 additional minute before seasoning with salt and pepper to taste.

Make it My Way

I like my green beans with a little bit of a snap. For tender green beans, cook on HIGH pressure for 0 minutes instead of LOW pressure.

Just the Basics

The ability to set the Instant Pot to 0 minutes is a little-known feature that can really come in handy for delicate vegetables like green beans.

SIDES

Notes

Creamed Corn

I will admit that canned cream corn was a guilty pleasure growing up, but I'm not sure there's actually any real dairy in those cans! Making it from scratch keeps all those warm and fuzzy feelings, while adding real flavor and a real creaminess that you can only get from fresh dairy.

Ingredients

2 tablespoons butter

1 small yellow onion, diced

¼ teaspoon dried thyme

4 cups frozen corn kernels

1¼ cups milk, divided

½ cup heavy cream

1½ tablespoons sugar

¾ teaspoon salt

¼ teaspoon pepper

2 tablespoons cornstarch

SAUTÉ | 15 MINUTES

1 Preheat the Instant Pot insert on SAUTÉ. Add butter and heat until sizzling.

2 Add onion and thyme and sauté for 3 minutes, just until onion is translucent.

3 Stir in corn and sauté for 5 minutes, until mostly defrosted.

4 Stir in 1 cup of the milk, heavy cream, sugar, salt, and pepper and, stirring constantly, bring up to a simmer.

5 Whisk cornstarch into the remaining ¼ cup of milk and stir into the creamed corn, bringing back up to a simmer. Stirring constantly, let cook 1 minute to thicken. Turn off cooker and serve.

Make it My Way

For a combination of textures, I like to remove ¼ of the creamed corn and blend it before adding it back in with the whole kernels.

Just the Basics

When cooking with milk, always be sure to stir all the way to the bottom of the pot and only simmer as long as you need to in order to thicken it before turning off the cooker.

SIDES

Notes

Zoodle Lo Mein

Zucchini noodles or "zoodles" make a great side for one of those days you just want to eat light. This Chinese takeout–inspired Zoodle Lo Mein is perfect to serve alongside Teriyaki Salmon (recipe page 141) or Hoisin-Glazed London Broil (recipe page 101). As this only uses the Instant Pot's sauté function, you can absolutely prepare this on the stovetop if your cooker is already busy preparing one of those other dishes.

Ingredients

3 zucchini, spiralized

Salt

1 tablespoon butter

1 tablespoon vegetable oil

¾ cup shredded carrots

½ cup thinly sliced yellow onion

2 teaspoons minced garlic

1 tablespoon soy sauce
  (tamari for gluten-free)

2 teaspoons light brown sugar

1 tablespoon sesame oil

SAUTÉ | 7 MINUTES

1 Place spiralized zucchini in a mesh strainer and lightly season with salt. Let stand 30 minutes as the salt pulls water out of the zucchini to drain. Toss to drain any additional water.

2 Preheat the Instant Pot insert on SAUTÉ. Add butter and vegetable oil and heat until sizzling.

3 Add carrots and onion and sauté for 3 minutes, just until onion is translucent.

4 Stir in spiralized zucchini and garlic and sauté 2 minutes.

5 Stir in soy sauce and brown sugar and sauté 1 additional minute or until zucchini is crisp-tender.

6 Turn off cooker and stir in sesame oil before serving.

Make it My Way

Spiralizing your own zucchini noodles is recommended, as I've found that the pre-spiralized noodles now sold in grocery stores can get mushy quickly.

SIDES

Just the Basics

The sesame oil is added after cooking as much of the flavor of sesame oil cooks out at a high heat.

Notes

Sous Vide Corn on the Cob

Using sous vide to prepare this corn on the cob is like marinating the corn in butter. The relatively low cooking temperature helps to break down the germ around the kernel without losing the bite of the kernel itself. If you need something on the table a little quicker, directions for steaming corn on the cob under pressure are also included below.

Ingredients

4 ears corn on the cob, shucked

¼ cup butter, chopped

¼ teaspoon salt

SOUS VIDE | 180°F | 40 MINUTES

1. Place steam rack at the bottom of the Instant Pot insert and fill with water to the MAX line. Place lid on Instant Pot.

2. Set Instant Pot to SOUS VIDE at 180°F for 40 minutes.

3. As the water preheats, place corn, butter, and salt in a vacuum-seal bag and seal.

4. Once water temperature is reached, submerge the bag in the water, secure lid on Instant Pot, and vent pressure valve to remain open. You may also cover with a glass lid.

5. For the best results remove and shake bag after the first 5 minutes to disperse the butter after it has melted.

6. Once cook time has elapsed, remove from bag to serve.

Steaming Corn on the Cob

To steam the corn under pressure, place 4 ears on a steam rack inside the Instant Pot insert. Pour in 1 cup of water or chicken stock. Secure and lock lid. Set to STEAM on HIGH pressure for 3 minutes. Carefully perform a quick release of the pressure and serve topped with butter and salt to taste.

Make it My Way

My daughter Caitlin and I love to put Bacon Salt (sold on QVC) on our corn on the cob!

Just the Basics

Frozen corn also can be prepared using this method without any changes to temperature or cook time.

SIDES

Notes

_____

_____

177

Butter-Poached Asparagus

Using the sous vide function on the Instant Pot allows you to perfectly poach asparagus in a small amount of butter with the aromatics of garlic and lemon cooked throughout. As asparagus is very delicate, the cook time is quick for a sous vide recipe, at only 10 minutes, making this a great side dish you can prep and vacuum seal in advance to just throw into the water bath right before dinner.

Ingredients

1 bunch thick asparagus, stalks trimmed by 2 inches

3 tablespoons butter, chopped

2 teaspoons minced garlic, optional

$\frac{1}{2}$ teaspoon lemon zest, optional

$\frac{1}{4}$ teaspoon salt

SOUS VIDE | 180°F | 10 MINUTES

1 Place steam rack at the bottom of the Instant Pot insert and fill the insert with water to the MAX line. Place lid on Instant Pot.

2 Set Instant Pot to SOUS VIDE at 180°F for 10 minutes for snappy asparagus and 20 minutes for very tender asparagus.

3 As the water preheats, place asparagus, butter, garlic, lemon zest, and salt in a vacuum-seal bag and seal.

4 Once water temperature is reached, submerge the bag in the water, secure lid on Instant Pot, and vent pressure valve to remain open. You may also cover with a glass lid.

5 For the best results, remove and shake bag after the first 5 minutes to disperse the butter after it has melted.

6 Once cook time has elapsed, remove from bag to serve.

Steaming Asparagus

To steam thick asparagus under pressure, place in a steam basket inside the Instant Pot insert. Pour in 1 cup of water, vegetable stock, or chicken stock mixed with garlic and lemon zest. Secure and lock lid. Set to STEAM on HIGH pressure for 1 minute. Carefully perform a quick release of the pressure and serve topped with butter and salt to taste. Be sure to remove cooked asparagus from the pot as soon as the cook time has elapsed, or it may overcook.

Just the Basics

Any amount of asparagus up to 1$\frac{1}{2}$ pounds can be cooked with this method, as some stores sell it by the bunch and others sell it in 1-pound bags.

SIDES

Notes

179

Pasta and Grains

pressure cook

Easy Mac and Cheese

This was the very first dish I ever made in an Instant Pot, and after that, I was sold! It was the creamiest mac and cheese I'd ever had, and I didn't even have to stand over the stove to constantly stir . . . or even drain the macaroni. For a full meal, try stirring in crumbled turkey bacon, lump crab meat, or cooked lobster and serving alongside a salad.

Ingredients

16 ounces elbow macaroni

4 cups chicken stock

1 tablespoon butter

2 cups shredded sharp
Cheddar cheese

1 cup shredded Colby-Jack cheese

1/2 cup grated Parmesan cheese

1/3 cup cream cheese, softened
(about 1/3 of an 8-ounce block)

Salt and pepper to taste

PRESSURE COOK | HIGH PRESSURE | 6 MINUTES | QUICK RELEASE

1 In the Instant Pot insert, stir to combine elbow macaroni, chicken stock, and butter.

2 Secure lid and seal pressure release vent.

3 Set Instant Pot to PRESSURE COOK on HIGH pressure for 6 minutes.

4 Once cook time has elapsed, carefully perform a QUICK RELEASE of the pressure.

5 Without draining any liquid, slowly stir in Cheddar cheese, Colby-Jack, Parmesan cheese, and cream cheese.

6 Let stand 2 to 3 minutes to thicken before seasoning with salt and pepper to taste.

Make it My Way

I always cook with Philadelphia brand cream cheese—not just to represent my hometown but also because I find it melts creamier than store brands.

Just the Basics

This can be made vegetarian by substituting vegetable stock or water in place of the chicken stock.

PASTA

Notes _____

_____

Vegetable Fried Rice

The RICE setting on the Instant Pot makes starting this Chinese fried rice as simple as it gets. I use frozen mixed vegetables to ensure that finishing the fried rice is just as simple! To be truthful, though, I actually find that the frozen vegetable medley, instead of fresh vegetables, reminds me more of classic Chinese takeout anyway.

Ingredients

2 cups long grain white rice, rinsed

2 cups vegetable stock

2 tablespoons soy sauce
(tamari for gluten-free)

1 tablespoon sesame oil

1/4 teaspoon ground ginger

2 tablespoons butter

2 tablespoons vegetable oil

2 large eggs, beaten

1 1/2 cups frozen mixed vegetables

Chopped scallions, for garnish

RICE | HIGH PRESSURE | LESS | NATURAL RELEASE

1 In the Instant Pot insert, stir together rice, vegetable stock, soy sauce, sesame oil, and ginger.

2 Secure lid and seal pressure release vent.

3 Set Instant Pot to RICE on HIGH pressure using the LESS preset.

4 Once cook time has elapsed, let the pressure release through NATURAL RELEASE for 10 minutes before quick releasing any remaining pressure.

5 Stir butter into rice before transferring to a large bowl or dish. Wipe down insert.

6 Set Instant Pot to SAUTÉ and add vegetable oil to the insert, heating until it thins out.

7 Pour the eggs into the insert and scramble until nearly firm. Stir in frozen vegetables and sauté 3 minutes.

8 Add the cooked rice to the vegetables and egg and sauté 4 minutes, constantly scraping the bottom of the pot to ensure that no rice is sticking.

9 Serve garnished with chopped scallions and alongside additional soy sauce, if desired.

Just the Basics

"Parboiled" long grain white rice (such as Uncle Ben's) works great in this recipe, as the grains don't stick together as easily. Just be sure not to use any "quick-cooking" or "minute" rice.

PASTA

Notes

Brown Rice with Cranberries and Pecans

A perfect alternative to stuffing around the holidays, this brown rice is a little sweet and a little nutty! Fresh sage, celery, and a hint of dried thyme really gives it that holiday stuffing flavor.

Ingredients

2 tablespoons butter

1 tablespoon vegetable oil

$3/4$ cup diced yellow onion

$3/4$ cup diced celery

$1 1/2$ cups long grain brown rice

$1 3/4$ cups vegetable stock

1 tablespoon chopped fresh sage

$1/2$ teaspoon salt

$1/4$ teaspoon pepper

$1/4$ teaspoon dried thyme

$1/4$ teaspoon onion powder

$1/2$ cup dried cranberries

$1/2$ cup chopped pecans

BEAN/GRAIN | HIGH PRESSURE | 20 MINUTES | NATURAL RELEASE

1. Preheat the Instant Pot insert on SAUTÉ. Add butter and vegetable oil and bring up to a sizzle.

2. Add onion and celery and sauté until onion is translucent, about 4 minutes.

3. Stir in brown rice and sauté 1 additional minute.

4. Pour in vegetable stock and deglaze the insert before stirring in sage, salt, pepper, thyme, and onion powder.

5. Secure lid and seal pressure release vent.

6. Set Instant Pot to BEAN/GRAIN or PRESSURE COOK on HIGH pressure for 20 minutes.

7. Once cook time has elapsed, let the pressure release through NATURAL RELEASE for 15 minutes before quick releasing any remaining pressure.

8. Fold in cranberries and pecans and let stand 5 minutes to soften cranberries before serving.

Just the Basics

Two teaspoons of dry rubbed sage can be used in place of the fresh sage. Ground sage is not recommended as it has a much earthier flavor, which I find more similar to cinnamon than an herb.

PASTA

Notes

Perfect White or Brown Rice

As a multicooker, the Instant Pot can replace a ton of other kitchen appliances, including a rice cooker. Whether it is white or brown rice, you can get perfect results every time, all while saving precious counter space by putting that rice cooker into storage!

Ingredients

WHITE RICE

$1\frac{1}{2}$ cups long grain white rice, rinsed

$1\frac{1}{2}$ cups water or stock

1 tablespoon butter or vegetable oil

$\frac{1}{2}$ teaspoon salt

BROWN RICE

$1\frac{1}{2}$ cups long grain brown rice, rinsed

$1\frac{3}{4}$ cups water or stock

1 tablespoon butter or vegetable oil

$\frac{1}{2}$ teaspoon salt

White Rice

RICE | HIGH PRESSURE | NATURAL RELEASE

1 In the Instant Pot insert, stir to combine rinsed rice, water or stock, butter or oil, and salt. Secure lid and seal pressure release vent.

2 Set Instant Pot to RICE on HIGH pressure using the LESS preset for perfectly al dente rice. For more tender rice, stir in an additional $\frac{1}{4}$ cup of water and use the NORMAL preset.

3 Once cook time has elapsed, let the pressure release through NATURAL RELEASE for 10 minutes before quick releasing any remaining pressure. Fluff with a fork before serving.

Brown Rice

BEAN/GRAIN | HIGH PRESSURE | 20 MINUTES | NATURAL RELEASE

1 In the Instant Pot insert, stir to combine rinsed rice, water or stock, butter or oil, and salt. Secure lid and seal pressure release vent.

2 Set Instant Pot to BEAN/GRAIN or PRESSURE COOK on HIGH pressure for 20 minutes.

3 Once cook time has elapsed, let the pressure release through NATURAL RELEASE for 15 minutes before quick releasing any remaining pressure. Fluff with a fork before serving.

Make it My Way

I always make my rice with chicken or vegetable stock in place of water for more flavor. I also love to add $\frac{1}{4}$ cup of chopped leeks to my white rice for a bit of color and onion flavor.

Just the Basics

With either type of rice, it's important that you let the pressure release naturally for at least 10 minutes, or it may end up sticking to the bottom of the pot.

PASTA

Notes

Risotto Primavera

This creamy risotto is bursting with colorful vegetables with very minimal prep work. This is as classic as a risotto gets by letting the flavors of white wine and Parmesan cheese shine.

Ingredients

3 tablespoons butter

$\frac{1}{2}$ yellow onion, diced

$\frac{1}{2}$ cup diced red bell pepper

1 tablespoon minced garlic

1$\frac{1}{2}$ cups Arborio rice

2 cups frozen mixed vegetables

3 cups vegetable stock

$\frac{1}{2}$ cup dry white wine

1 bay leaf

$\frac{1}{2}$ teaspoon salt

$\frac{1}{2}$ teaspoon pepper

$\frac{1}{2}$ cup heavy cream

$\frac{1}{2}$ cup grated Parmesan cheese

Chopped parsley, for garnish

PRESSURE COOK | HIGH PRESSURE | 5 MINUTES | QUICK RELEASE

1 Heat butter in the Instant Pot insert on SAUTÉ.

2 Add onion, bell pepper, and garlic and sauté for 3 minutes, just until onion is translucent.

3 Stir in rice and sauté 1 additional minute before stirring in mixed vegetables, vegetable stock, white wine, bay leaf, salt, and pepper.

4 Secure lid and seal pressure release vent.

5 Set Instant Pot to PRESSURE COOK on HIGH pressure for 5 minutes.

6 Once cook time has elapsed, carefully perform a QUICK RELEASE of the pressure.

7 Stir in heavy cream and Parmesan cheese before serving topped with chopped parsley.

Make it My Way

White wine is wonderful in risottos; however, you can substitute $\frac{1}{2}$ cup of additional vegetable stock and 2 teaspoons of lemon juice, if desired.

Just the Basics

Risottos will thicken as they stand, and you will likely need to add additional vegetable stock or cream to thin them out to your desired consistency just before serving. Using stock is best, as it will not water down the flavor.

PASTA

Notes

Creamy Herbed Cheese Polenta

Polenta is a creamy Italian dish made from coarse ground yellow corn in the same way that Americans make grits in the South. Just be sure to find cornmeal that is specifically labeled "coarse" or "polenta" and steer clear of anything that says it is "quick cooking" or "instant," as that will be over-processed and not nearly as delicious as the real thing.

Ingredients

1 cup coarse cornmeal (polenta)

4 1/4 cups chicken stock

2 teaspoons minced garlic

6 ounces herbed cream cheese

1/4 cup milk

2 tablespoons grated
  Parmesan cheese

Salt and pepper to taste

Chopped fresh parsley, for garnish

PORRIDGE | HIGH PRESSURE | 10 MINUTES | NATURAL RELEASE

1 In the Instant Pot insert, stir to combine cornmeal, chicken stock, and garlic.

2 Secure lid and seal pressure release vent.

3 Set Instant Pot to PORRIDGE on HIGH pressure for 10 minutes.

4 Once cook time has elapsed, let the pressure release through NATURAL RELEASE.

5 Stir in herbed cream cheese, milk, and Parmesan cheese before seasoning with salt and pepper to taste.

6 As the polenta will thicken quickly, you may wish to thin it out with additional milk or chicken stock just before serving. Serve topped with chopped fresh parsley, if desired.

Make it My Way

This makes the perfect side dish to serve under any stewed or roasted meat, especially meats with gravy that can mix right into the polenta.

Just the Basics

This can be made vegetarian by substituting vegetable stock or water in place of the chicken stock.

PASTA

Notes

Southwestern Mac and Cheese

One mac and cheese recipe in this book was not enough for me (and probably not my friend David Venable)! This Southwestern take is made with only a few simple ingredients, like salsa, frozen corn, and taco seasoning, to pack your weeknight with flavor, not prep work.

Ingredients

16 ounces corkscrew
  pasta or cavatappi

3 1/2 cups vegetable stock

1 cup chunky salsa

3/4 cup frozen corn kernels

1 tablespoon olive oil

1 tablespoon taco seasoning

2 cups shredded pepper
  Jack cheese

1 cup shredded sharp
  Cheddar cheese

1/2 cup sour cream

Salt and pepper to taste

PRESSURE COOK | HIGH PRESSURE | 5 MINUTES | QUICK RELEASE

1 In the Instant Pot insert, stir to combine pasta, vegetable stock, salsa, corn, olive oil, and taco seasoning.

2 Secure lid and seal pressure release vent.

3 Set Instant Pot to PRESSURE COOK on HIGH pressure for 5 minutes.

4 Once cook time has elapsed, carefully perform a QUICK RELEASE of the pressure.

5 Without draining any liquid, slowly stir in pepper Jack cheese, Cheddar cheese, and sour cream.

6 Let stand 2 to 3 minutes to thicken before seasoning with salt and pepper to taste.

Make it My Way

For even more Southwestern flair, add 3/4 cup of canned black beans (drained and rinsed) before pressure cooking.

Just the Basics

Sometimes I get lucky and find pepper Jack cheese that is pre-shredded in a bag, but I often have to just shred it myself. An 8-ounce block is equal to the 2 cups in this recipe.

Notes

Baked Ziti

This has everything you love about a baked ziti casserole.... Without any of the actual baking! The ziti is cooked right in the tomato sauce before stirring in creamy ricotta cheese. Melted mozzarella cheese tops this one-pot casserole off without having to heat up your whole kitchen.

Ingredients

16 ounces ziti pasta

3 3/4 cups vegetable stock

1 (24-ounce) jar pasta sauce

1 tablespoon olive oil

2 teaspoons minced garlic

3/4 teaspoon Italian seasoning

1 cup ricotta cheese

1/2 cup grated Parmesan cheese

Salt and pepper to taste

1 cup shredded mozzarella cheese

PRESSURE COOK | HIGH PRESSURE | 5 MINUTES | QUICK RELEASE

1 In the Instant Pot insert, stir to combine ziti, vegetable stock, pasta sauce, olive oil, garlic, and Italian seasoning.

2 Secure lid and seal pressure release vent.

3 Set Instant Pot to PRESSURE COOK on HIGH pressure for 5 minutes.

4 Once cook time has elapsed, carefully perform a QUICK RELEASE of the pressure.

5 While still hot, quickly stir in ricotta and Parmesan cheeses before seasoning with salt and pepper to taste.

6 Top with the mozzarella cheese and secure the lid in place for 3 minutes with the cooker off, just to melt the cheese before serving.

Make it My Way

Instant Pot is releasing their new Air Fryer Lid that can be used to actually brown the cheese on the top by setting to BROIL for 3 minutes or just until cheese begins to brown.

Just the Basics

The pasta may be slightly al dente after pressure cooking, but it will continue to cook as the mozzarella cheese melts.

PASTA

Notes

Barley and Mushroom Pilaf

Barley is one of those great grains that I never took the time to cook with before I had my Instant Pot. It just seems to take forever on the stove and still ends up a bit too chewy for my liking. While barley is always going to be a little "toothsome," this savory pilaf with mushrooms has just the right bite, thanks to the fact that no steam can escape when cooking under pressure.

Ingredients

1 tablespoon olive oil

2 tablespoons butter

8 ounces baby bella mushrooms, quartered

1/2 cup diced yellow onion

1/2 cup diced celery

2 teaspoons minced garlic

1 cup pearled barley

2 1/4 cups beef stock (may use vegetable)

1 sprig fresh thyme

1 bay leaf

Salt and pepper to taste

1/4 cup chopped pecans

BEAN/GRAIN | HIGH PRESSURE | 20 MINUTES | QUICK RELEASE

1. Preheat the Instant Pot insert on SAUTÉ. Add olive oil and butter and bring up to a sizzle.

2. Add mushrooms, onion, celery, and garlic to the pot and sauté until onion is translucent, about 4 minutes.

3. Stir in barley and sauté 1 additional minute.

4. Pour in beef stock and deglaze the insert before stirring in thyme and bay leaf.

5. Secure lid and seal pressure release vent.

6. Set Instant Pot to BEAN/GRAIN or PRESSURE COOK on HIGH pressure for 20 minutes.

7. Once cook time has elapsed, carefully perform a QUICK RELEASE of the pressure.

8. Remove lid, discard thyme and bay leaf, and let rest at least 3 minutes to thicken before seasoning with salt and pepper to taste. Serve topped with chopped pecans.

Make it My Way

I love to cook with College Inn brand stocks and broths. I'll use broths for dishes where I want a lighter flavor and stocks for dishes like this one, where I want more of a punch.

Just the Basics

Be sure to purchase "pearled" or "pearl" barley, not "instant" or "quick cooking" as those are more processed, not as good, and don't require this long of a cook time.

PASTA

Notes

195

Caramelized Carrot Risotto

This lightly sweet, but mostly savory, risotto is loaded with the flavor of butter-caramelized carrots. It's great as a main course all on its own—or try topping it with roasted meat or vegetables.

Ingredients

3 tablespoons butter

1/2 yellow onion, diced

2 cups shredded carrots, divided

1 1/2 cups Arborio rice

1/4 teaspoon ground nutmeg

3 1/2 cups vegetable stock

4 ounces garden vegetable cream cheese spread

3 tablespoons maple syrup

1 1/2 tablespoons light brown sugar

1/4 teaspoon salt

1/4 teaspoon pepper

PRESSURE COOK | HIGH PRESSURE | 5 MINUTES | QUICK RELEASE

1 Heat butter in the Instant Pot insert on SAUTÉ.

2 Add onion and 1 cup of the carrots and sauté for 5 minutes or until carrots are tender and butter is beginning to lightly brown.

3 Stir in rice and nutmeg and sauté 1 additional minute before stirring in vegetable stock.

4 Secure lid and seal pressure release vent.

5 Set Instant Pot to PRESSURE COOK on HIGH pressure for 5 minutes.

6 Once cook time has elapsed, carefully perform a QUICK RELEASE of the pressure.

7 Stir in cream cheese spread, maple syrup, brown sugar, salt, pepper, and the remaining 1 cup of shredded carrots and let rest 2 minutes before serving.

Make it My Way

I like to use the "garden vegetable" flavor of cream cheese spread (Philadelphia brand) to add even more flavor; however, regular cream cheese also can be used if you prefer.

Just the Basics

Risottos will thicken as they stand, and just before serving, you will likely need to add additional vegetable stock, milk, or even water to thin them out to your desired consistency. Using stock is best, as it will not water down the flavor.

Notes _____

_____

Desserts

pressure cook

(V) Classic Cheesecake, 201

(V) Peach Bread Pudding with Caramel, 203

(🌾) (V) White Chocolate and Tangerine
Rice Pudding, 204

(🌾) (V) Black Cherry Sundae Syrup, 205

(V) Tropical Paradise Cake, 207

(V) Key Lime Pie, 209

(V) Banana Nut Bread, 210

(🌾) (V) Spiced Apple Cider, 211

(V) Mom's Butter Rice Pudding, 213

(V) Peanut Butter Chocolate Lava Cakes, 215

sous vide

(🌾) (V) Cranberry Poached Pears, 217

DESSERTS

199

Classic Cheesecake

The steam environment inside of the Instant Pot is the perfect place to make a cheesecake, as the dry heat of an oven can dry the cake out. With this recipe, you'll get creamy results every time! I like to serve my cheesecake topped with Black Cherry Sundae Syrup (recipe page 205).

Ingredients

Nonstick cooking spray

$^3/_4$ cup graham cracker crumbs

3 tablespoons butter, melted

2 tablespoons light brown sugar

16 ounces cream cheese, softened

$^2/_3$ cup sugar

$^1/_4$ cup heavy cream

2 large eggs

1 large egg white

1 tablespoon cornstarch

1$^1/_2$ teaspoons vanilla extract

ACCESSORIES

7-inch springform pan

PRESSURE COOK | HIGH PRESSURE | 1 HOUR | NATURAL RELEASE

1 Spray a 7-inch springform pan with nonstick cooking spray.

2 In a mixing bowl, combine graham cracker crumbs, melted butter, and brown sugar to create the crust.

3 Firmly press the crust into the bottom of the springform pan. For best results, place in freezer for 30 minutes.

4 In an electric mixer, beat all remaining ingredients just until smooth. Pour over the chilled crust and tap on counter to flatten out the top and remove any air bubbles.

5 Fully wrap and cover the springform pan in aluminum foil to prevent any water from seeping into the bottom of the pan.

6 Pour 1 cup of water into the Instant Pot insert. Place wrapped springform pan on a steam rack and lower into the cooker. Secure lid and seal pressure release vent.

7 Set Instant Pot to CAKE or PRESSURE COOK on HIGH pressure for 1 hour.

8 Once cook time has elapsed, let the pressure release through NATURAL RELEASE.

9 Let cheesecake cool on counter for 1 hour, then refrigerate at least 4 hours before slicing to serve.

Just the Basics

I like to change the aluminum foil on the top of the pan after cooking, as a lot of steam builds up inside of it and will eventually drip back down onto the top of the cheesecake.

Notes

DESSERTS

Peach Bread Pudding with Caramel

This bread pudding is loaded with chopped peaches and topped with a sweet caramel sauce. Rum extract and sweetened condensed milk help accentuate the flavors of both the peaches and the caramel. For the perfect topping, serve with a scoop of peach ice cream!

Ingredients

Nonstick cooking spray

5 large eggs

3/4 cup sweetened condensed milk

1/2 cup heavy cream

1/2 teaspoon rum extract
  (may use vanilla)

1/4 teaspoon ground cinnamon

Pinch salt

5 thick slices brioche bread

1 cup frozen peaches,
  thawed and chopped

Caramel syrup, to top

ACCESSORIES
7-inch springform pan

PRESSURE COOK | HIGH PRESSURE | 45 MINUTES | NATURAL RELEASE

1 Spray a 7-inch springform pan with nonstick cooking spray. Fully wrap the outside and bottom of the pan to prevent leaking.

2 In a large mixing bowl, whisk together eggs, condensed milk, heavy cream, rum extract, cinnamon, and salt.

3 Fold bread and peaches into the egg mixture. For best results, let stand 15 minutes.

4 Transfer the bread and egg mixture to the prepared pan and cover tightly with aluminum foil.

5 Pour 1 cup of water into the Instant Pot insert. Set the springform pan on a steam rack and lower into the cooker.

6 Secure lid and seal pressure release vent.

7 Set Instant Pot to PRESSURE COOK on HIGH for 45 minutes.

8 Once cook time has elapsed, let the pressure release through NATURAL RELEASE.

9 Let cool 10 minutes before slicing or spooning into bowls to serve drizzled with caramel syrup.

Just the Basics

Be sure to drain the thawed peaches well before chopping and adding to the pudding. I like to pat them dry with paper towels.

DESSERTS

Notes

White Chocolate and Tangerine Rice Pudding

Rice pudding is made even creamier by melting white chocolate right into it before serving. Tangerine zest then adds a contrasting zing that gives this an irresistible Creamsicle-like flavor.

Ingredients

1½ cups medium grain rice

2½ cups water

⅔ cup sugar

½ cup fresh tangerine or orange juice

Zest of 1 tangerine

1 tablespoon butter

1 teaspoon vanilla extract

1 large egg

1 cup whole milk

½ cup white chocolate chips

PRESSURE COOK | HIGH PRESSURE | 6 MINUTES | NATURAL RELEASE

1 In the Instant Pot insert, stir to combine rice, water, sugar, tangerine juice, tangerine zest, butter, and vanilla extract.

2 Secure lid and seal pressure release vent.

3 Set Instant Pot to PRESSURE COOK on HIGH pressure for 6 minutes.

4 Once cook time has elapsed, let the pressure release through NATURAL RELEASE for 10 minutes before covering vent with a towel (the steam could be sticky) and quick releasing any remaining pressure.

5 Whisk egg into milk and then quickly whisk in a few tablespoons of the hot cooked rice to temper the egg. Stir this tempered egg mixture into the rice in the insert.

6 Stir in white chocolate chips before serving topped with additional tangerine zest, if desired.

Make it My Way

Believe it or not, I think the tangerine zest in this is much more flavorful than the orange zest, but the zest of a medium orange can be substituted in a pinch.

Just the Basics

The rice should be hot enough after cooking to heat the egg to a safe temperature, but if you would like to be safe, you can set the Instant Pot to SAUTÉ on LESS and heat, stirring constantly, for 3 minutes, just until steaming hot.

DESSERTS

Notes

Black Cherry Sundae Syrup

This simple sundae syrup is made from scratch without the corn syrup and artificial flavors you'd find in store-bought dessert sauces. I find that a tiny splash of vanilla extract perfectly complements the cherries, but it can be omitted if you'd prefer.

Ingredients

16 ounces frozen cherries

$1/4$ cup water

$1/8$ teaspoon vanilla extract

$1/3$ cup sugar

1 tablespoon cornstarch

2 tablespoons cold water

PRESSURE COOK | LOW PRESSURE | 1 MINUTE | NATURAL RELEASE

1 Place frozen cherries, water, and vanilla extract in the Instant Pot insert. While this seems like very little liquid, the cherries will release plenty of liquid as the pot comes up to pressure.

2 Secure lid and seal pressure release vent.

3 Set Instant Pot to PRESSURE COOK on LOW for 1 minute.

4 Once cook time has elapsed, let the pressure release through NATURAL RELEASE.

5 Set Instant Pot to SAUTÉ and stir in sugar.

6 Whisk cornstarch into 2 tablespoons of cold water and, stirring frequently, add to the cooked cherries. Bring up to a simmer and stir, just until thickened. Immediately turn off cooker.

7 Cover and refrigerate at least 1 hour before serving.

Make it My Way

This is perfect to serve over my Classic Cheesecake (recipe page 201) but is also great over ice cream, oatmeal, or yogurt.

Just the Basics

Make sure the pressure has fully released naturally before opening the pressure release vent, as the cooked cherries will be very thick and could splatter from the vent if they are still under pressure.

Notes

DESSERTS

Tropical Paradise Cake

This yellow Bundt cake has pineapple and coconut mixed in for an even more tropical flavor than your typical Pineapple Upside-Down Cake. I've found that using a 7-inch Bundt pan makes for the largest cake possible in a 6-quart Instant Pot.

Ingredients

Nonstick cooking spray

1/2 cup pineapple juice

1/4 cup canned pineapple chunks, plus 5 chunks for the pan

2 large eggs

3 tablespoons vegetable oil

2 tablespoons butter, melted

1/4 teaspoon coconut extract

2 cups yellow cake mix (see Just the Basics)

5 maraschino cherries, rinsed

Shredded coconut, for garnish

GLAZE

1 cup powdered sugar

2 tablespoons pineapple juice

1/2 teaspoon vanilla extract

ACCESSORIES

7-inch Bundt pan

CAKE | HIGH PRESSURE | 40 MINUTES | NATURAL RELEASE

1 Spray a 7-inch Bundt pan with nonstick cooking spray.

2 In a blender, blend pineapple juice, 1/4 cup pineapple chunks, eggs, vegetable oil, butter, and coconut extract until smooth. Add the cake mix and blend just until all is combined.

3 Alternate the 5 extra chunks of pineapple with the 5 maraschino cherries at the bottom of the prepared pan. Pour the batter into the pan and tap on the counter to even out the top.

4 Fully wrap the bottom and top of the Bundt pan in aluminum foil to ensure it is watertight.

5 Pour 1 cup of water into the Instant Pot insert. Set the Bundt pan on a steam rack and lower into the cooker.

6 Secure lid and seal pressure release vent.

7 Set Instant Pot to CAKE or PRESSURE COOK on HIGH pressure for 40 minutes.

8 Once cook time has elapsed, let the pressure release through NATURAL RELEASE.

9 Let cool completely before serving drizzled with glaze and topped with shredded coconut, if desired.

Preparing the Glaze

Use a fork to whisk together all Glaze ingredients until smooth. If the glaze is too thick, add additional pineapple juice a teaspoon at a time. If the glaze is too thin, add additional powdered sugar.

Just the Basics

A standard (15.25-ounce) box of yellow cake mix contains 3 cups of mix. Two boxes can prepare this recipe 3 times.

DESSERTS

Notes _____

_____

Key Lime Pie

You don't have to go all the way to Key West to get a slice of this tart custard-filled pie. An extra-thick graham cracker crust helps cut some of the tartness in the filling, making for a sweet escape, made in only 20 minutes under pressure.

Ingredients

Nonstick cooking spray

1 cup graham cracker crumbs

¼ cup butter, melted

2 tablespoons light brown sugar

4 large egg yolks

1 (14-ounce) can sweetened condensed milk

½ cup key lime juice

¼ teaspoon vanilla extract

¼ cup sour cream

Zest of 1 lime

ACCESSORIES

7-inch springform pan

PRESSURE COOK | HIGH PRESSURE | 22 MINUTES | NATURAL RELEASE

1 Spray a 7-inch springform pan with nonstick cooking spray.

2 In a mixing bowl, combine graham cracker crumbs, melted butter, and brown sugar to create the crust.

3 Firmly press the crust into the bottom of the springform pan. For best results, place in freezer for 30 minutes.

4 In a clean mixing bowl, whisk egg yolks, condensed milk, key lime juice, and vanilla extract until fully combined. Fold in sour cream and lime zest to finish the filling.

5 Pour the filling over the chilled crust and tap on counter to flatten out the top and remove any air bubbles. Fully wrap and cover the springform pan in aluminum foil to prevent any water from seeping into the bottom of the pan.

6 Pour 1 cup of water into the Instant Pot insert. Place wrapped springform pan on a steam rack and lower into the insert. Secure lid and seal pressure release vent.

7 Set Instant Pot to PRESSURE COOK on HIGH for 22 minutes.

8 Once cook time has elapsed, let the pressure release through NATURAL RELEASE.

9 Remove aluminum foil and let pie cool on counter for 1 hour, then cover and refrigerate at least 4 hours before slicing to serve.

Just the Basics

Key lime juice is sold in small unrefrigerated bottles that are sometimes in the fruit juice aisle and sometimes in the produce section (near bottles of lemon juice).

Notes

DESSERTS

Banana Nut Bread

This super-moist banana bread is prepped easily by using a premade mix but tastes homemade thanks to the addition of two whole bananas and chopped walnuts. Cooking under pressure gives it a dessert-like, almost creamy texture, rather than the crumbly muffin-like texture of baked banana bread.

Ingredients

Nonstick cooking spray

2 small bananas, peeled

½ cup milk

2 large eggs

3 tablespoons sugar

4 drops yellow food coloring, optional

1 (7.6-ounce) pouch banana nut muffin mix

¼ cup chopped walnuts

ACCESSORIES

6.5-inch springform loaf pan

CAKE | HIGH PRESSURE | 1 HOUR | NATURAL RELEASE

1 Spray a 6.5-inch springform loaf pan with nonstick cooking spray.

2 In a blender, blend bananas, milk, eggs, sugar, and food coloring until smooth.

3 Fold in muffin mix and walnuts until all is combined into a batter.

4 Pour the batter into the prepared pan and tap on the counter to even out the top. Fully wrap the pan in aluminum foil to ensure it is watertight.

5 Pour 1½ cups of water into the Instant Pot insert. Set the springform pan on a steam rack and lower into the insert. Secure lid and seal pressure release vent.

6 Set Instant Pot to CAKE or PRESSURE COOK on HIGH pressure for 1 hour.

7 Once cook time has elapsed, let the pressure release through NATURAL RELEASE.

8 Let cool at least 15 minutes before slicing to serve.

Just the Basics

The yellow food coloring in this is optional but recommended because the fresh bananas will darken as the bread cooks, making the bread slightly gray if the yellow coloring isn't added. Either way, it has no effect on taste!

Make it My Way

I make this with Martha White brand Banana Nut Muffin Mix. Other brands have different amounts of batter and may not work as intended.

DESSERTS

Notes _____

_____

Spiced Apple Cider

Warm apple cider is a wonderful escape from a Pennsylvania winter! The Instant Pot allows you to make cider from fresh apples, while infusing it with the spice of whole cinnamon sticks and cloves. I like to toss in 1 orange for even more flavor and a bit of "zest."

Ingredients

6 large apples

1 orange

8 cups water

3 cinnamon sticks

½ teaspoon whole cloves

½ cup light brown sugar

PRESSURE COOK | HIGH PRESSURE | 15 MINUTES | NATURAL RELEASE

1. Core and coarsely chop the apples, without peeling, into large pieces, adding to the Instant Pot insert as you go.

2. Cut the orange, without peeling, into wedges and add to the insert.

3. Pour water over fruit and ensure the fruit is fully covered, adding additional water if necessary.

4. Stir in cinnamon sticks, cloves, and brown sugar, stirring until sugar has dissolved.

5. Secure lid and seal pressure release vent.

6. Set Instant Pot to PRESSURE COOK on HIGH pressure for 15 minutes.

7. Once cook time has elapsed, let the pressure release through NATURAL RELEASE for 15 minutes before quick releasing any remaining pressure.

8. Remove cinnamon sticks and use a potato masher to fully mash the fruit into the cider.

9. Strain the cider through a fine mesh strainer before serving cider warm or chilled.

Make it My Way

For an adult party, you can spike this cider with bourbon to taste for a truly warming holiday beverage.

Just the Basics

Any variety of apples can be used to make this, and it is an especially good recipe for using up a bag of apples that are starting to bruise.

Notes

DESSERTS

Ⓥ

Mom's Butter Rice Pudding

My mother never actually made rice pudding, but my daughters still can't stop talking about Grandma's amazing Butter Tart. While that recipe is a custard pie that truly requires baking in an oven, I've taken all of the ingredients and combined them into this rice pudding. It has all of the same flavors of maple syrup, brown sugar, butter, egg, and raisins, presented in a way that you can eat with a spoon. I even dip shortbread cookies into it to replicate her buttery pie crust!

Ingredients

1½ cups medium grain rice

3 cups water

¾ cup raisins

½ cup dark brown sugar

¼ cup maple syrup

¼ cup butter

½ teaspoon maple extract

Pinch salt

1 large egg

1 cup whole milk

Shortbread cookies, to serve

Just the Basics

The rice should be hot enough after cooking to heat the egg to a safe temperature, but if you would like to be safe, you can set the Instant Pot to SAUTÉ on LESS and heat, stirring constantly, for 3 minutes, just until steaming hot.

PRESSURE COOK | HIGH PRESSURE | 6 MINUTES | NATURAL RELEASE

1 In the Instant Pot insert, stir to combine rice, water, raisins, brown sugar, maple syrup, butter, maple extract, and salt.

2 Secure lid and seal pressure release vent.

3 Set Instant Pot to PRESSURE COOK on HIGH pressure for 6 minutes.

4 Once cook time has elapsed, let the pressure release through NATURAL RELEASE for 10 minutes before covering vent with a towel (the steam could be sticky) and quick releasing any remaining pressure.

5 Whisk egg into milk and then quickly whisk in a few tablespoons of the hot cooked rice to temper the egg. Stir this tempered egg mixture into the rice in the insert.

6 Serve warm with whole or crumbled shortbread cookies over top.

Make it My Way

I like to make this with medium grain rice as it cooks up creamier, releasing more starch, than long grain rice. Any medium grain rice will work, even Arborio rice, which is typically used for risottos.

DESSERTS

Notes _____

Peanut Butter Chocolate Lava Cakes

I think we all know that a molten center makes any cake better and that peanut butter is meant to go with chocolate! These mini chocolate cakes know both of these facts, and that is why they have an irresistible molten peanut butter center.

Ingredients

Nonstick cooking spray

3 large eggs

1/2 cup sugar

1/4 cup all-purpose flour

1 cup dark chocolate chips

1/2 cup butter, chopped

2 tablespoons smooth peanut butter

ACCESSORIES

4 (6-ounce) ramekins

Just the Basics

To fit 4 ramekins in the Instant Pot at the same time, you may have to place 3 of them in a triangular pattern with the fourth sitting atop where those intersect.

PRESSURE COOK | HIGH PRESSURE | 8 MINUTES | QUICK RELEASE

1 Spray ramekins with nonstick cooking spray.

2 In a mixing bowl, whisk eggs and sugar until creamy before folding in flour.

3 In a separate bowl, microwave chocolate chips and butter in 30-second increments, stirring between each, just until melted and smooth. Do not overcook.

4 Fold the melted chocolate mixture into the egg mixture until all is combined into a batter. Pour batter into each ramekin until each is about halfway full. You should still have remaining batter.

5 Spoon 1/2 tablespoon of the peanut butter into the center of the batter in each ramekin before covering with an equal amount of the remaining batter.

6 Pour 1 cup of water into the Instant Pot insert. Place uncovered ramekins on a steam rack and lower into the insert. Secure lid and seal pressure release vent.

7 Set Instant Pot to PRESSURE COOK on HIGH for 8 minutes.

8 Once cook time has elapsed, carefully perform a QUICK RELEASE of the pressure. Unlock and lift lid off quickly and without turning to the side to ensure water collected in the lid doesn't drip onto the cakes.

9 Use silicone tongs to remove ramekins. If water has collected on the tops of the cakes, gently dab with a paper towel. Run a knife around each cake to release and invert onto a plate to serve.

Make it My Way

I like to serve these sprinkled with powdered sugar, with a fresh mint leaf and raspberries for garnish.

DESSERTS

Notes

215

Cranberry Poached Pears

While often made in red wine, these pears are poached in sweet and tangy cranberry juice for a family-friendly take on an elegant and simple dessert. Cooking them sous vide allows ample time for the cranberry flavor to soak in without overcooking the pears.

Ingredients

2 ripe pears
1/2 cup cranberry juice
1/4 cup light brown sugar
1/2 teaspoon orange zest

SOUS VIDE | 175°F | 1 HOUR

1. Place steam rack at the bottom of the Instant Pot insert and fill the insert with water to the MAX line. Place lid on Instant Pot.

2. Set Instant Pot to SOUS VIDE at 175°F for 1 hour.

3. As the water preheats, peel, halve, and core the pears. Place in a vacuum-seal bag.

4. Whisk together cranberry juice, brown sugar, and orange zest and pour over the pears. Seal bag.

5. Once water temperature is reached, submerge the bag in the water, secure lid on Instant Pot, and vent pressure valve to remain open. You may also cover with a glass lid.

6. Once cook time has elapsed, remove from bag and serve warm, drizzled with liquid from the bag.

Make it My Way

I like to serve this topped with vanilla ice cream, but it is also good with whipped cream (Cool Whip holds up to the warm pears better than real cream).

Just the Basics

Any type of large pears will work in this recipe. It makes for an especially nice presentation if you find pears with the stem on.

Notes

Index

Acknowledgments

I would like to thank all the wonderful people that were instrumental in helping me get to this point to write and publish this cookbook.

To my family, Chris, Caitlin, and Heather, thank you for your continuous support over the years with my crazy QVC early mornings and late-night hours and your honest opinions of my recipe taste tests—good, bad, or indifferent. I am so grateful for your strength and encouragement, especially when I doubt myself. Your support and belief in me mean more than I could ever express, and I love each of you from the bottom of my heart.

I would like to thank my Instant Pot Facebook family (all 2 million of you!) for being part of such a wonderful, sharing community. I am grateful for my QVC and HSN families. I am privileged to work alongside talented and giving QVC Program Hosts like David Venable, Mary DeAngelis, Stacey Stauffer, Antonella Nester, and Carolyn Gracie, to name a few. In addition to the Program Hosts, I am blessed to work with caring and supportive "foodie friends," who guest other wonderful products at QVC.

A big "Thank you" to Mamey and Adam, the QVC/HSN buyers who unknowingly encouraged me to write this cookbook. You realized there was a need for an all-encompassing Instant Pot cookbook that provided mouth-watering meals as well as tips and tricks for getting the most from the Instant Pot. In my search for such a book, I realized that to find it, I had to create it, and I am so grateful and appreciative for the opportunity to share my insights and recipes.

There are two people who I will be eternally grateful for in this endeavor. Sheila Thomas, with my publisher, Quail Ridge Press, and Christian Stella, whose continued support and expertise in this field were above and beyond my expectations. Together, they have brought this cookbook to life, and without them, this book would not have come to fruition. It has been a goal of mine to not only share my easy, delicious recipes but also to provide others with tips on how easy and fun it is to use the Instant Pot Pressure Cooker! This is my first cookbook, and without Sheila's guidance and patience, I would not have been able to pull this off! She was instrumental in many, MANY aspects of this book, but I am particularly appreciative of everything she did in setting up and organizing the chapter opener shots. Being able to actually shoot these in my own home—in the very kitchen in which these recipes were created—was a dream come true!! Sheila worked tirelessly to make sure everything was perfect and that we captured all the love and excitement in each shot.

Christian, a true artist, and perfectionist, helped to make sure the recipes were correct, the photograph for each recipe was amazing, and the book's design and layout were not only beautiful but also user-friendly and easy to read! All of this was crucial to the development and completion of this cookbook. I could never have imagined a pot roast could look so delicious on the page (and it tastes just as delicious as it looks)! Most of all, I am grateful for Sheila and Christian's friendship, and I am truly appreciative of their support, dedication, and hard work to help make this cookbook come to life.

My final "Thank you" is to YOU (yes, you, the reader!) for opening your home and your heart to my recipes and advice. I hope that using your Instant Pot will bring you amazing meals, wonderful memories, and less time cleaning and cooking! My Instant Pot has turned preparing and sharing meals into a time of bonding and building memories. I truly hope your Instant Pot and this cookbook will do the same for you and your loved ones!

Warmly,

Lisa

QVC Culinary Expert/On Air Spokesperson and product development expert **Lisa Brady** was born and raised in a small town outside of Vancouver, in British Columbia, Canada. From a large family with seven siblings, Lisa realized her love of cooking at an early age, while watching and helping her mom cook family meals.

At seventeen, Lisa started working in restaurants as a cook. Before long, she was managing and opening numerous new locations for the same locally owned family brand. In 1985, she took a much-deserved extended vacation to visit her sister, who was living in Pennsylvania, USA. Lisa had planned to return to her career as a restaurant manager, when she met Chris Brady. The two married and later settled down outside of Philadelphia with their two daughters, Caitlin and Heather. Lisa managed local restaurant chains outside of Philadelphia for several years prior to taking a break from the industry to raise her children.

In 2004, Lisa's zesty personality, restaurant experience, and love of cooking brought her to QVC, the world's largest live-shopping channel. Lisa focused on kitchen items, introducing products such as the Instant Pot to QVC families across the nation. The impact of the Instant Pot on Lisa's life was significant. It was a life-changing product that helped her make delicious, quality meals within modern-day time constraints. Many have asked Lisa for her recipes, tips, and tricks, so this cookbook was born to satisfy those requests. It is her pleasure to share her favorite meal experiences with you.

Follow Lisa Brady on social media for more recipes and tips:

Instagram: @LisaBradyQVC and @BrunchinBradys
Facebook: Lisa Brady QVC
Twitter: @LisaBradyQVC